— THE —

24/7

SOLUTION

"Emily's experience, success, and commitment to the home care industry shines through in *The 24/7 Solution*. Her ability to explain the 'why' and the 'how' creates a clear roadmap towards growth and financial sustainability. Home Care seems simple from the outside, but to grow multiple offices year over year, owners must have a plan. *The 24/7 Solution* identifies tools, processes, and solutions that assure future success to anyone willing to put in the work."

– Jennifer Bassett, Home Instead franchise owner

"Emily understands the challenges facing home care agency owners, particularly franchisees, and meets them with empathy – and accountability. This book provides not just the blueprint, but the coaching and motivation owners need to increase both their profits and their personal time."

– Kristen Duell, Executive Vice President of Experience & Innovation at FirstLight Home Care, Founder of IDEAL for Healthcare, McKnight's 2024 Agent of Change honoree, and recipient of Aging Media's 2023 40 under 40 award

"As a fellow home care entrepreneur, I found Emily Isbell's *The 24/7 Solution* to be an amazing resource for anyone in the home care industry. Blending personal anecdotes with practical advice, it offers insightful strategies for growth and operational excellence. Her methodical approach to establishing a rhythm of accountability through annual, monthly, and weekly meetings, along with end-of-day check-ins, mirrors the practices that have driven success in my own organization. This book is not just an informative read; it's a journey towards transformative leadership and work-life harmony while working in the home care industry."

– Ryan Iwamoto, President & Co-Founder of 24 Hour Home Care

"Emily Isbell's book *The 24/7 Solution: Proven Strategies for Home Care Business Leaders* revolutionizes the home care industry by addressing challenges at their core – leadership. Isbell emphasizes self-leadership, urging leaders to recognize their role in agency success. The book explores emotional intelligence, often overlooked in business, emphasizing understanding, and managing emotions within the team. Isbell promotes empathy over excuses, encouraging leaders to acknowledge challenges while fostering growth. The metaphor of being a thermostat, not a thermometer, guides leaders to set the temperature amid challenges. With practical advice and a focus on personal growth, Isbell's book is a transformative guide for home care leaders, offering a profound shift in perspective for the entire industry."

– Bob Roth, Managing Partner, Cypress HomeCare Solutions

"As a home care business owner, it's a go-to guide on how to operate and grow a business in this space. The fact that Emily can speak to this from a practiced and proven standpoint is very meaningful. She has taken ideas that my business partner and I have thought about for a long time and outlined a process to make implementing them easy and trackable."

– Franny Schmidt, Touching Hearts Franchise Owner

"From my time working with Emily Isbell at Home Instead, she has proven to be a mission-driven, dedicated, passionate leader who achieves incredible results from her teams and her businesses. The leadership approach and best practices she built from her experiences growing and leading large profitable businesses and that she shares in *The 24/7 Solution* are valuable to leaders throughout home care and beyond. Home care is a simple business model but difficult to execute well. The learnings and strategic tools that Emily shares in her book create a roadmap to help light our path on this journey of providing care to older adults everywhere."

– Jisella Dolan, Founder and CEO of One For the Ages and global leader in home care

"Emily has written a must-read for home care agency owners or anyone considering becoming one. Read this book – and learn from one of the best in the industry. This practical guide is full of easy-to-implement tactics to grow any home care business to new heights."

– Denise DiSano, Founder and CEO of enCappture Home Care, Crain's Notable Women Business Owner

"Finding a resource as effective as this is quite rare. It not only guides you towards success but also allows you the valuable time to enjoy your achievements. Emily's experience in running and scaling profitable businesses offers immense practical value to entrepreneurs aiming for greatness. *The 24/7 Solution* is an essential read for anyone seeking to improve their business."

– Aaron Stromley, CEO of Touching Hearts at Home

"Emily's journey is a remarkable tale of perseverance and dedication, setting a high bar in the homecare industry. With over thirty years of experience in this field, I am impressed by the substantial impact she has made in just fourteen years. Her book, *The 24/7 Solution: Proven Strategies for Home Care* is an indispensable resource, offering a pragmatic and intelligent approach to managing a homecare business. It's not just a guide for the majority of homecare owners, be they part of a franchise or independent; it's a vital read for every team member within the homecare sector. Emily's book transcends the typical business manual. It serves as a unifying tool that aligns team members, management, and ownership, fostering a cohesive and efficient operation. In an industry that is rapidly evolving, *The 24/7 Solution* emerges as a pioneering work, offering fresh insights and strategies crucial for navigating the complexities of modern homecare services. It's a testament to what the industry needs now and a beacon for those striving for excellence in this vital field."

– Jeff Salter, Founder and CEO of Caring Senior Service

"If you want to get your time back and be a better leader as a home care owner, then *The 24/7 Solution: Proven Strategies for Home Care Business Leaders* is a must read. Emily shares her inspiring personal experiences and ties bite-sized action items and proven strategies you can do into them so you can improve the operations of your home care business."

– Andrew Dahle, COO of Assisting Hands Home Care

"It takes remarkable courage to start a business from scratch. Work ethic and determination to conquer the learning curve. Nerves of steel during that time between start and positive cash flow. Too often, the person who overcomes all these obstacles to build a profitable business becomes the bottleneck to sustained growth. While her story plays out in the home care industry, the lessons Emily imparts would be useful for any entrepreneur looking to get out of their own way."

– Michael Slupecki, CEO of Griswold

"Emily's message connected with me both as an agency owner since 2007 in Beaverton Oregon and a franchisor since 2020. I can tell you from firsthand experience that she has tapped into real challenges for not only an operator who might be launching an office, but equally serves those offices trying to breakthrough to the next revenue target, customer service improvement, or team development. Our collective mission as an industry is to improve the lives of aging adults and the caregivers that serve them. Emily's roadmap helps us all get there!"

– Clayton W. Foutch, Founder and COO of Home Matters Caregiving, Board member HCAOA, Chair Beaverton Committee on Aging

"If you prefer to do it yourself, then go. Do it. Yourself. But if you prefer to maximize viability for your homecare agency via specialized and proven systems, then leverage Emily's repeatable experience and success. Her *The 24/7 Solution: Proven Strategies for Home Care Business*

Leaders reveals wisdom to minimize setbacks often associated with DIY trial and error."

– Bruce Berglind CEO, SwyftOps Homecare Operating Software, Former ComForCare Franchisee

"Emily Isbell has written a much-needed guide to delivering on the promises of home care that all leaders, regardless of where they are in their journey, will find valuable. *The 24/7 Solution* provides clear, action-oriented responsibilities that leaders must embrace to develop the full potential of themselves, their teams and their organizations."

– Susan Richardson, Empowering Potential Consulting, Former VP of Learning and Development at Home Instead

"Prepare to be empowered! In *The 24/7 Solution: Proven Strategies for Home Care Business Leaders*, Emily Isbell seamlessly combines practical, no-nonsense insights with real-world examples that breathe life into the daily struggles and triumphs of owners in the home care industry. This book is a must read for anyone seeking not only to survive but to thrive in the competitive landscape of the home care sector. Ms. Isbell draws from her wealth of personal experience, providing invaluable tools and techniques that will truly elevate your business."

– Linda Young, CEO and Founder of LYC Inc.

"If you have challenges running your business – this book is for you! You'll learn practical strategies and tactics for creating efficiencies that will greatly enhance your business and build a loyal following in the workplace. A must-read to overcome obstacles, reach your full potential, and find the right balance between your personal and professional life."

– Phyllis Hegstrom, Former Government Affairs Director at Home Instead

"When it comes to the issue of the work-life balance of small business leaders, Emily Isbell offers sound counsel as both a wise instructor and an experienced practitioner. Relying on her own life experience as a business owner and business coach, Emily lays out sensible, practical solutions for business leaders struggling to manage their commercial enterprises and their personal lives. This book is essential reading for anyone interested in creating a healthy lifestyle while running a successful, productive business."

– David Surbaugh, retired publishing executive

"I've had the good fortune to be in the room as Emily put into practice many of the strategies in this book. She is one of the best I've seen at making order out of chaos – taking the available facts, opinions, and sometimes strong emotions, and distilling them into actionable steps for real results. This book isn't just about setting lofty goals for years down the road. It's about the practical steps you can take today, this week, or this month to begin a journey toward having the business you want to have, being the employer your staff wants to work for, and delivering the kind of compassionate care so often lacking in the industry. Oh, and you can do it all without burning yourself out! Emily is a proven producer *and* an incredible human being. Heed her advice if you, too, would like to become both!"

– Adam Mosley, entrepreneur

"*The 24/7 Solution* is a must-read book for anyone wanting to make an impact or change in their business. With Emily's words, packed full of interesting anecdotes, personal experience, and thoughtful quotes, it feels more like you are having lunch with a long-time friend rather than reading a book!"

– Mollie Hanrahan, small business owner

"The 24/7 Solution is a must read for anyone in the home care industry. It is direct and solution-focused to create life altering change not only for your business but your work/life balance. This book will help you reclaim your life from your work!"

– Megan Harden, LCSW, CEO

"Although *The 24/7 Solution* was written to address the ever-growing home care industry, I found the techniques, business practices, and strategies adaptable to almost any field where there is a need for individuals to take ownership (and pride) in their work. I can see applications and tools useful for many businesses large or small that rely heavily on the importance of both client service and sales for future growth."

– Mary M. Kelly, MBA, financial consultant

"The unique combination of passion, dedication, and expertise is what Emily Isbell brings to the table. As an expert in the field, her credentials speak for themselves; however, her commitment and attention to detail sets her apart. Working alongside her in a non-home health-care space, I have witnessed first-hand the person who has assessed, created processes, identified, and managed areas in desperate need of improvement, while offering concrete ways to implement the strategies that had been identified to ensure future success. She is a consummate professional and exceptionally knowledgeable. The concrete wisdom and resources offered in this book are foundational to anyone in the industry wishing to identify, strategize, and implement solutions and solve problems in their own business. She is a leader who, combined with her passion for this sector, shares the tools necessary to be successful with those wishing to grow and learn."

– Lori Macmath, fellow non-profit board member

"Emily has hit the nail on its head with this book. Having been in the industry for over a decade I can say that this is a must read for anyone looking to venture into the market. She outlines the importance of soft skills and by reading this you can fast track the experience needed for success and scale."

– Amrit Dhaliwal CEO and Founder of Walfinch

THE

24/7

SOLUTION

Proven Strategies for
Home Care Business Leaders

EMILY ISBELL

Publishing support provided by
Ignite Press
55 Shaw Ave. Suite 204
www.IgnitePress.us
Clovis, CA 93612
www.IgnitePress.us

ISBN: 979-8-9901845-0-3
ISBN: 979-8-9901845-1-0 (E-book)

For bulk purchases and booking, contact:
Emily Isbell
emily@eiandcompany.com
www.eiandcompany.com

The content of this book is based on the experiences of Emily Isbell and her time
completing home care turnarounds both as a franchisee and today with her clients.
Individual business results may vary.

Library of Congress Control Number: 2024903816

Cover design by Miladinka Milic
Edited by Elizabeth Arterberry
Interior design by Jetlaunch

FIRST EDITION

To my grandmother. While I helped serve thousands of seniors across multiple states, I missed out on time serving you. Even though I wish I had lived closer to you, when I look back, I am thankful for every phone call you made to encourage me in the work I was doing. I can hear you now: "That's my girl."

ACKNOWLEDGMENTS

I would like to acknowledge my book coach, Cathy Fyock, for her practical approach that allowed me to get this book written quickly without sacrificing quality. She also gave invaluable feedback on the initial draft to help me make this book what it is today.

I would like to also acknowledge the editorial board who took the rough cut and helped me smooth out all of the edges: Linda Young, Sara Thomsen, Juanita Almy, and Jessi Skidmore.

I would also like to acknowledge the team at Ignite Press. You have been instrumental in helping me get across the finish line without breaking a sweat. Thank you for making this process so easy.

And, finally, our nanny, Ashley. Without your flexible support on weekdays and weekends, this book would have never been accomplished. Thank you for providing my son with a safe and loving space during my absence.

THANK YOU

A special thank you to Lori and Paul Hogan, the founders of Home Instead, for following their passion to help other seniors flourish the same way Grandma Manhart was able to flourish.

Further thank you to Brad and Amy Cannon for having faith in their entrepreneurial abilities and opening the Home Instead franchise that hired me as a caregiver, as well as for the continued mentorship and opportunities you provided for me that allowed me to go from caregiver to Vice President of Operations of multiple units during my fourteen years at Home Instead.

Last, and most importantly, my Co-Leader™ and wife – Tara. You are a huge part of why I am where I am today. Your encouragement since 2012 has been the secret ingredient to my tenacity. Thank you for helping me continue to grow and become a better person every day. I remember saying to you in the first months of knowing you, "dream big," to which you followed up, "there is no other way to dream." Everyone needs a Tara in their life.

TABLE OF CONTENTS

FOREWORD

J.J. Sorrenti, CEO of Best Life Brands

I have been fortunate enough to be directly involved in helping more than 5,000 small business owners get into business through franchising in different industries and categories. Each of those individuals started with the dream of being in business for themselves, and while they did not all have the same goals, the common theme was that they wanted to be successful in business. Some were even more successful than they imagined. Some achieved their goals and moved on. However, a few were not as successful as they thought they could be, which frustrated them – and us.

Each of those business owners, especially the most successful ones, was always on the lookout for simple and practical advice to help them reach their potential. Often, the best guidance was found during simple discussions about the everyday activities of the business. Sure, we knew and understood the business we were leading, whether it was selling supplements, helping students succeed in school, or taking care of aging seniors. Often, the best improvements for a small business owner were strict discipline and the practical execution of just one or two ideas, or "hacks," involving the use of a simple roadmap to make the employees more effective, increasing revenues and profits.

That is where Emily Isbell comes in. It is not often you meet someone who has been doing something for over sixteen years with an intense passion to do even more of it. Usually, after all those years, there is burnout and fatigue. As you learn about her background, you will realize, like I did, that she has a caring heart, and is always searching for something bigger – to make a bigger impact. So, when you learn about and apply the roadmaps built in this book, not only will you have a much greater chance to realize your own potential, you will also be helping her achieve her goal of helping as many people as possible.

By reading this book, you are taking the first step to unlocking your own potential and the potential for your business's success. Now, open your mind and learn more about the practical and easy to execute ideas that will help make it happen – thanks to Emily Isbell and her *24/7 Solution.*

INTRODUCTION

"Tell me more about you," I said to a potential client in the early days of my business.

"My franchisor considers me a leading franchisee; every new owner is told about how I have grown incredibly fast and is encouraged to call me when they have a question. I've received awards at every conference since I purchased a franchise. I'm a go-getter and very competitive."

Perplexed, given the client's confident response, I wondered aloud, "Okay, so why are we meeting today?"

"I'm honored and happy to help other franchisees, but what my franchisor doesn't understand is I'm in debt up to my ears, I never get to have a day off, and I'm barely able to pay myself. I'm grateful to help other franchisees grow revenues, but I barely have time to go to the dentist. They haven't been able to help, and they continue to remind me how incredible my revenues are. The revenues don't lead to getting a healthy income or having any time off. I really need help. I don't know how much longer I can continue."

This was a surprising meeting for me. I expected this owner's experience to be an anomaly – a top performing franchisee exhausted, crippled by significant debt with minimal profit and an inability to find balance. I expected to find common difficulties among the franchise owners and franchisors I helped, but did not expect to work with so many with such similar stories.

Although each client I have worked with has had a unique story and set of needs, they shared a common thread, one unique to the mission of those called to work in the home care industry: owning a business that truly cares for and gives back to others, primarily the seniors of our communities. My own desire to be a business owner and help seniors has driven my career and inspired me to share my experiences and knowledge in this book. Maybe you, too, have a similar pull to serving in the senior home care industry.

In 2007, I began as a caregiver with Home Instead Senior Care in a college town in Kentucky. I was two semesters shy of completing my bachelor's degree in psychology when I worked my first shift with a client. I remember that client so well. He was an elderly gentleman who had been diagnosed with Alzheimer's disease. His short-term memory was severely limited. During the three hours we spent together, we discussed his siblings no less than twenty times. Each time, the number of siblings he shared changed: first three, then four, then eight. His delight and pride in sharing overshadowed the difficulties of his disease. I immediately fell in love with the idea that I was able to brighten his day with my presence and simple conversation. I knew I wanted to make a career for myself that facilitated more of those moments.

Shortly after my first visit with this client, I went to the Home Instead website and filled out the "Inquire to be a Franchisee" questionnaire. Little did I know it was an application, and a nineteen-year-old college student was far from a viable prospect. At the time, ownership was clearly out of reach, so, instead, I reached out to the local Home Instead owner and asked him how I could one day sit in his chair. He was immediately receptive to my very forward question and quickly became the mentor I hadn't known I was seeking. From that meeting, he encouraged me to consider a degree in Health Care Administration and, without making any promises of ownership that he couldn't keep, he simply stated, I can help you."

By 2012, I had risen to second in command of that Home Instead location. We were serving upwards of 20,000 hours a month in care, and I had agreed to continue to work together with the owner rather than pursuing individual ownership on my own. Our agreement was simple: he would put forward the capital to purchase an additional territory while I contributed the sweat equity, building and managing operations there. As one of the top franchisees at the company, we were confident in our plans. We sent our pitch to Home Instead's global headquarters and began looking at the available territories for sale. We made a list and were ready to start researching where I would end up moving.

A few days later, the owner pulled me into his office with a look of disappointment and said, "They said no."

I responded, very confused, with "Who?"

"The home office. They want to stick to their core formula of owners not having multiple territories and ensuring that the owner has a local presence in the territories they own."

"Well then, they need to meet me!"

The owner smirked at my confidence. "Let me call them and see."

It wasn't long before we had a flight booked and an hour blocked for me to speak to the senior leadership team of the global headquarters for Home Instead, Inc. My audience was to include the founders and C-suite executives, all of whom had a lot more experience than my twenty-four-year-old self. Suddenly, reality was sinking in. It was now my job to convince experts of a globally successful home care brand that I wasn't the typical new college graduate. I needed to assure them I was committed to caring for a community in the same way an owner would, and that I was worth betting on. It was a tall order to face that room full of pedigree and experience. I was nervous, intimidated, and worried I wouldn't be perceived as good enough. Despite this, I never questioned my ability to succeed.

As we arrived in Omaha, Nebraska, we were greeted warmly and given a tour of the global headquarters. The Global Operations portion of the building was the most inspiring. I remember noticing the clocks on the wall, with each clock set to display the local time of a country that Home Instead franchises served. I thought of Ms. P, one of our 24/7 clients, who at that very moment was likely having her breakfast prepared. I noted the clock for Japan read 11:00 p.m. I envisioned a Ms. P in Japan being tucked back into bed for the night after her caregiver helped her safely to and from the restroom. Contemplating the global reach of the work I did and desperately wanted to continue to flourish within was both comforting and incredibly humbling. The weight of convincing the leaders of this global brand that I was fit to lead a franchise began to feel heavier.

Next, we had lunch with several of the leaders, including the COO, Dave Banark. Dave and I made a connection through a fondness for similar authors from across the scale, such as Malcolm Gladwell and Eckhart Tolle. Sitting next to Dave at that lunch felt like the universe's way of saying, "You got this; these people are not that different from you."

That afternoon, I conducted my presentation. I remember very little of the presentation itself, but can vividly recall my closing remark. I summed up my presentation with a favorite quote from Van Gogh: **"Your profession is not what brings home your weekly paycheck, your profession is what you were put here on earth to do, with such passion and such intensity that it becomes spiritual in calling."**

Then the team began to ask me questions.

"How do you plan to manage your time?"

"What do you do to alleviate stress?"

They were all questions I was prepared to answer, until one of the owners, John Hogan, asked, "What one word would the owner use to describe you?"

One word?! I hesitated, thinking to myself, *this needs to be good. What one word will inspire them to believe in me?*

I stalled, saying, "Two words come to mind, and I'm struggling to pick just one."

In truth, hundreds of words were swirling in my mind.

"I'm not sure what one word he would use because I think there are many, but I will pick the one that I believe he would agree with, and one that I received as an award when I was a competitive gymnast – dedicated. I was awarded 'Most Dedicated Gymnast' one year, and that trait is a core value of mine to this day."

After we wrapped up and I could finally breathe again, I spoke with the owner and learned they had, in fact, asked him to use one word to describe me. His answer? Committed.

Three days later, the owner pulled me into his office and excitedly shared, "They said yes!"

I'm not sure I even acknowledged him; all I can remember was getting to my car as quickly as possible and driving to "get lunch."

Sitting at a stoplight away from the office, I broke down in happy tears and sat there in such disbelief. I had earned the opportunity and was excited to take on the challenge.

Over the next few years, there were seasons where tears were a regular occurrence, and they were far from happy. At a particularly low point in early 2016, I almost called it quits. Although I was earning a very healthy income, I had no time away from work to even spend it. The owner and I discussed selling and began entertaining offers. I recall giving one potential buyer a tour of the office and thinking about all the next steps I would need to take to make sure I left the office in the best shape possible. *I really need to demote this team member. She's an incredible human being, but she isn't fit for the role she's in. It wouldn't be fair to give the new owners that situation.*

I fielded questions about business operations and, after answering, found myself planning improvements to implement prior to selling. *I better fix how on-call is managed so they can sustainably keep this business running as owners and still spend time with their children.* After the tour, I had a phone call with the owner. The possibility of selling was weighing heavily on both of us. He reflected on a recent conversation with another Home Instead owner, where that owner stated, "There is no other business where you have the opportunity to earn such an incredible income, provide incredible jobs, and serve seniors the way we have here."

That night, I went to sleep developing the plan for the office – demote her, implement this, update this process, and so on, all for the future owners. By the next morning, I woke up and said, "Why not do this for myself?"

If I could fix it for them, I could fix it for me.

Like a lightning bolt striking me, I realized I didn't have to give up the incredible income, the amazing service we provided, and continue to lose my time away from the office. If I could fix it for them, I could fix it for me. We contacted the buyers with the disappointing news that afternoon.

Later that same year, we purchased a second territory and I became the face of two units and two separate leadership teams. I worked part-time in each unit as their leader, and both businesses grew tremendously. And, by the way, I went on a trip every quarter with my spouse and rarely worked a fifty hour plus work week again.

Fast forward to eight years later and the systems I had put in place to manage multiple sites led to the acquisition of seven franchises, serving over one million hours of care a year across three states.

A common misconception is that the more territories you run, the easier it is. As home care owners hear the "CliffsNotes" version of my story, they immediately believe more is better, that the reason success came was because we acquired more businesses and size provides you with more opportunities to solve problems. That is far from the truth. In fact, the businesses would have crumbled if the solutions I implemented to systemize our processes had not occurred.

Maybe you are having challenges with the 24/7 pull of the business. Is that why you were drawn to this book? Was it because you want to scale your business up and build leaders within your organization? Has the eighty hour work week run its course? Or was the last complaint from a client's daughter your final straw? My hope for you is that this book will help you find the same "24/7 Solution" I was able to find for my businesses.

HOW TO READ THIS BOOK

Over the course of this book, you will learn about the "24/7 Solutions" I put in place that led to my success. I often joke that putting everything I did over the course of my career into a book would require an entire encyclopedia set. There are so many nuances to a successfully-run home care agency, but this book contains the foundation. This foundation allows you to begin building an organization that systematizes performance improvements that lead to more efficient practices, better care, increased service hours, and increased profits. And, by the way, this means you start working a balanced schedule again.

My company, EI & Company, has a logo that contains a cloud; this symbol is inspired by the adage "keep your head in the clouds, but your feet on the ground." To get to multiple profitable, efficiently-run home care businesses, you have to dream big and have your head in the clouds. However, you must be just as grounded in reality.

As you read this book, you may become overwhelmed by the long list of things you realize you need to do for your business. How I choose to look at it is that there are two boxes of action items: action items directly assigned within this book, and action items you'll pick up by simply reading stories about how we handled certain matters. To avoid being overwhelmed or feeling that this is too much to handle, I would advise this: keep a list of action items of "nice to have" versus "need." Any of the items I instruct you to do, I consider a "need" in your business. Any good ideas you come across naturally would be "nice to have."

When it comes to the "nice to have" list, here's my advice. Pick three things from that list to do right now. Just three. Once you've accomplished those three things, return to your list and pick three more. As I compiled these sections, I started with what I believed needed to occur first to help readers build the best foundation. However, as I always tell my clients, you know *your* business better than I do or ever can, so if the first step I offer doesn't make sense for your business, move on to the next. Any process improvement you make today will only continue to serve your business tomorrow.

Any process improvement you make today will only continue to serve your business tomorrow.

If you are the type to read a book entirely before putting it down, you may want to reconsider that approach for this book. To help you digest the material and apply solutions in your business, I have suggested stopping points. When you see the **24/7 Solution Time** icon:

24/7 SOLUTION TIME

I am recommending you stop reading, implement the related suggestion or concept in your organization plan, and schedule a deadline via a one-hour meeting with yourself. When the deadline is met, utilize that calendar block of one hour to review your work and recalibrate by asking yourself these questions:

1. Did I complete my goal?
2. What went well in the implementation of this step?
3. What didn't go so well?
4. What can I do differently to improve the results of this step?

5. Do I need to extend my deadline by a few weeks to accomplish this step?
    a. If so, when is my next "24/7 Solution Time" scheduled?
    b. Did I update my calendar?

For a link to a worksheet with these questions, go to www.the-247solution.com, download the *24/7 Solution Time Worksheet*, and attach it to your digital calendar block.

Once you run through this exercise, at the time of the deadline, either schedule a follow-up deadline or pick up this book and continue reading. The reflection exercise above will likely take fifteen to twenty minutes, and the remaining time on the calendar can be used to take action based on question number four, or to continue reading this book to learn about the next steps you need to implement.

Word of caution to those who want to read this in entirety before acting: be sure to look in the mirror and ask yourself...

"...am I wanting to read this cover to cover because I'm afraid to take action? If I'm afraid to take action based on a proven model, is that the reason my business isn't where I want it to be? **Am I on the verge of meeting with a seller, and able to list all the things they should do in the business to succeed, but unwilling to do them myself?**"

If you want to read the book in its entirety, I'll say to you what I say to all of my clients: the choice is ultimately yours, and your business' success lies in your hands. Be aware that you may find yourself procrastinating, and your business' results suffering. If this is the case, you may want to reach out to us at EI & Company and schedule a consultation so we can help you get started.

As already referenced in this section, you will see portions throughout this book that recommend you visit www.the247solution.com. You will still be able to gain a great deal of value without downloading tools from this site because many of the recommended steps to take in your business are provided within this book. However, through uploading additional resources to this site, I am able to bring you even more value. It is important to note that some of these tools require an investment. Most tools are complementary for those who have purchased this book, but a few highly valuable resources will require payment in order to be downloaded.

Lastly, make note of references I make throughout these pages. I intentionally name a lot of experts that have come before me and individuals worth studying as I put together the information on these pages. It has been said, a leader is a reader. Where possible, take note of the books you can read or listen to and see if there is even more that can be applied to your home care career than what I have been able to condense down into these pages.

1

SELF-LEADERSHIP

In the same way I had to realize the changes started with me, you will need to have this realization, too. What is your potential seller moment? Having the "24/7 Solution" work for your home care business starts with you. The issue isn't the high demand and low supply, the issue isn't that the state regulations are too rigid, the issue isn't that your administrative team won't follow instructions, or that no one can afford private care. Just like it was with me, the issue is with *you*, to start. If you're not ready to accept this as true, that is okay. I invite you to continue reading, as I am confident you will still find many nuggets to apply to your business.

Self-Reflection

A common practice in business is to debrief. A debrief, according to Oxford Dictionary, "is a series of questions about a completed mission or undertaking." In the instructions concerning how to read this book, I've already asked you to begin to apply this practice to your leadership. Now, I am letting you know how this exercise can apply far beyond a project or job. If we remember that it all starts with us then we need to look in the mirror and debrief our actions on a regular basis. Beyond utilizing the "24/7 Solution Time" debrief for completing tasks within this book, I recommend using this self-reflection exercise.

1. What did I do well?
2. What did I not do so well?
3. What will I do differently next time?

These three questions, asked in this order, are a key part of self-leadership and growth. If you are not willing to take this step, you are not willing to grow, just as Jon Beaty put it in his book, *If You're Not Growing, You're Dying*. The book hits on a place we frequently find ourselves in during different stages of life: getting stuck in a neutral phase – think the same kind of "neutral" as the one found on a vehicle's gearshift. Beaty goes on to describe that, if you're not growing, then you are going to start rolling backwards quickly.

The idea of being stuck in a neutral space is an illusion. You likely know this better than anyone. As a home care owner, you cannot get complacent. As soon as you think revenues are stable, a client passes away. As soon as you believe your team is a team of loyal all-stars, someone's moving three states away to take care of a family member. That is why these three questions are so vital to your business, your growth as a leader, and your revenues.

Take a moment and print this self-reflection exercise document from www.the247solution.com. Better yet, print many. One for your home mirror, one for your computer monitor, one for your dashboard, heck, even put one by the toilet paper holder at home. Immerse yourself in this practice. Remember how I said everything starts with you? By the end of this book, your team will be applying this same practice to their work. As a leader, we never want to ask our team to do something we won't do ourselves.

Emotional Intelligence

Brené Brown once said, "We like to think we are rational beings who occasionally have an emotion and flick it away, and carry on being rational. But, rather, we are emotional, feeling beings; who, on rare occasions, think." I have to work diligently to remember quotes; it is not a strength of mine. I tend to mix up idioms and am notorious for saying "that's the icing on the camel's back." However, Brown's quote has never left my mind. As I listened to that interview, I think she even surprised herself by how profound of a statement she made.

As a woman, it has always irritated me to hear other women say "well that's a man for you" as they excuse a man from not taking a moment to be considerate towards someone else. Similarly, I have always been bothered by men who are quick to say that a woman is responding emotionally. As the comedian Hannah Gadsby once pointed out, she has known quite a few men to be "a little testy." Regardless of the obvious differences between men and women, what I am ultimately trying to say is:

1. We are all human beings, and, as human beings, we all have emotions.
2. We are all human beings, and, as human beings, we are all capable of being thoughtful about how we affect another human being.

I continue to meet men and women alike who own businesses in the home care industry and are unaware of their lack of emotional intelligence. *Emotional intelligence* is the ability to manage both your own emotions and understand those of the people around you. Regardless of your sex, you are driven by emotions – you are an emotional being. That is what makes the human race such a spectacular wonder compared to many other species.

Anthropologist Margaret Mead was once asked by a student what she considered to be the first signs of civilization. Those listening anticipated that she would point to the creation of tools for hunting, or pots for cooking, but, instead, Mead said the first signs were a 15,000 year old fractured femur found at an archeological site.

The femur, being the longest bone in the body, takes around six weeks of rest to heal. This 15,000 year old bone was not only fractured – it had healed. In the animal kingdom, Mead explained, if you become this injured, you die. No creature survives a broken leg long enough for it to heal. For this bone to have healed, it meant that another person chose to stay with the injured individual and provide them safety until they recovered. This ultimately meant that we had evolved into a species that was able to put others' care ahead of or equal to our own survival. Along with the emotional capacity for empathy came all of the other emotions we carry: greed, jealousy, sadness, anger, joy, contempt, and so on.

Many business owners lack knowledge about how their own emotions guide their decisions. Then they compound this ignorance with a lack of awareness of the emotions of those they lead and serve. Their naïveté regarding emotions is what leads to the death of their business. This lack of intelligence shows up in different ways for different people.

For some owners, this manifests as them working themselves to the bone serving clients and employees and barely ever sleeping. Their time with family will continue to be sacrificed, and, before they know it, they're in a hospital recovery room healing from a major life-saving surgery. For others, they will continue to move along the narcissism spectrum, starting off confident, only to become arrogant, surrounding themselves with yes-people who are too scared to tell them the truth about their blind spots. While they may be successful in revenue gains, their lack of emotional intelligence will lead to team members who get in over their heads and say "yes" to their bad ideas, and to fighting lawsuit after lawsuit from clients, employees, and the government. If they don't fall into either of those categories, those others generally find themselves filing for bankruptcy.

Those are the end results when you lack awareness and fail to educate yourself on and evolve your emotional intelligence. Learning about your emotional intelligence doesn't look like an annual planning meeting with yourself to evaluate your past year and determine whether you've evolved. Instead, this skillset is made stronger day in and day out. If you find yourself being pulled into the emotional whirlwind of the day, your business' results will continue to remain stagnant. On the other hand, if you are naïvely "turning off your emotions" and ignoring the temperature of the team's moods, you will have the exact same results – stagnating, once again. There is a delicate balance to strike when determining the appropriate amount of emotional reaction versus cerebral reaction in a given situation.

Here is the good news: you will get stronger, and it will become less and less exhausting. Since 2020, I have worn a scales of justice charm on a small silver necklace around my neck. When people take note, they ask if I'm a lawyer, or a libra, and, every time, I have to explain that I am neither. The scales of justice don't even represent justice to me. These scales are my reminder to hold everything in balance, especially my emotions and the emotions of those around me.

I teach my clients an approach I have coined: "Embrace empathy over excuses." A key part of success in team building is utilizing this concept. Embracing empathy over excuses is the opposite of having sympathy and allowing responsibilities and commitments to be ignored. Many leaders show sympathy when their team members are struggling. They feel they are acting out of love by allowing team members to disregard responsibilities and commitments during a time of personal struggle.

In other words, sympathy, for them, is looking the other way and understanding that you cannot fully know what the person is dealing with, so it's best to hug them, say you're sorry about their situation, and move on. As you continue to look the other way, other team members get hurt, take on unfair workloads, drop the ball with clients, and then leave suddenly due to burnout or frustration. As the owner of your business, you are doing eighty hours of work or more, not sleeping well at night, and clients are unhappy. Why is this happening? It is because of *sympathy*, allowing excuses to derail the plans and expectations you have set as an organization.

To embrace empathy over excuses, you acknowledge an individual's difficulties, put yourself in their shoes, and then you work *together* to maintain their responsibilities and commitments to the business.

When leaders look the other way, deep down, they feel they are being empathetic to the person and their situation, but what they are really doing is preventing that individual from growing. Additionally,

> **When leaders look the other way, deep down, they feel they are being empathetic to the person and their situation, but what they are really doing is preventing that individual from growing.**

they are preventing other team members, their own leadership skills, and their business from growing.

The key part of embracing empathy over excuses is that you do not completely ignore the excuses you are given. You recognize the excuses and seek a middle ground that still allows the team member and the business to achieve the results set forth.

When I was a competitive gymnast, I suffered a hairline fracture on my right ankle during the off season. Although the break was small, it still required me to stay on crutches for nearly three weeks, and in a cast for eight weeks. There was no way I was going to be practicing my beam routine in a cast. Instead of staying home for those eight weeks because I had an excuse, my coach met me with empathy and developed a specialized training plan. I continued with my four day a week, four-hour-long practices with my team, with my coach adapting every skill so that I could continue to improve as a gymnast. When the cast came off, I had to rehabilitate my right leg and get it caught up in strength, but when competition time came around, I won my first ever all-around gold medal!

Had my coach interacted with me from a place of sympathy and encouraged me to rest during those eight weeks, I would have never won that gold medal. Owners believe meeting their team members with sympathy is the "nice" thing to do, and they are right. It is "nice." But it is not kind. If your team member is struggling to keep up in their role because of trouble at home, you may be tempted to be nice to them and let the rest of your team pick up their slack. However, being nice has a shelf life. Being kind is sustainable. To be kind, you would take the time to understand their situation and meet them where they are, recognize their challenges, and then remind them of their goals at work and the results you expect from them.

You don't stop there, though. When you remind them of these results, you don't simply say, "Now go get 'em, tiger! You got this!" No, you sit side by side with them and ask them how you can help get them there. How, *together*, you can make it possible for them to still achieve their goals despite their challenges.

Ultimate Responsibility

My experience with my coach provides a great example of a leader embracing empathy over excuses, helping me to grow as a gymnast. It also exemplifies an incredible level of ultimate responsibility taken on by my coach and my middle school self. Here is part of the story I didn't share. My ankle broke during a fun relay game on the uneven bars. It wasn't while practicing a routine or doing some magnificent trick. It happened because I was rushing to get out of my teammates' way.

My teammate, Lisa, was both enthusiastic and aggressive in her tone as she yelled at me to "hurry up." I dismounted and landed halfway on, halfway off a mat. In a split second, my ankle yelled a very loud "nope!"As my teammate continued to yell at me to get out of the way, I rocked back and forth in gut-wrenching pain. The details after that are hazy, but I'll never forget the look of my black and blue, softball-sized ankle.

My coach called to check in on me the next day and was quick to take the blame for the injury. She felt awful for having us play a silly relay game and not having equipment set up properly for the race. Her remorse was palpable. Instead of saying to me that I failed to dismount properly (which I did), she took ultimate responsibility for my injury and followed up with a detailed plan outlining how we would keep me in shape and ready for competition season even with this setback.

Similarly, I didn't go back to practice and blame my teammate for my broken ankle, resentful over the thought that, had she not yelled at me, I would be able to practice and get ready for competition season. Instead, I recognized my failed dismount, made a mental note to never do that again, and decided to do what I could and trust my coach when it came to staying conditioned and competition-ready.

The concept of ultimate responsibility provides the benefit that, with any problem you may face, directly or indirectly, you can be a part of the solution. My coach was indirectly involved with my ankle fracturing; she didn't rush the dismount causing me to land poorly, *I* did. Even so, she took ultimate responsibility for the part she played in my healing journey, recognized the circumstances, and helped me succeed in spite of my situation. This, combined with her empathy (not sympathy), is what allowed me to grow and finally become an all-around gold medal gymnast.

Thermostat

Perhaps you have heard the saying, "be the thermostat, not the thermometer." This is one of the most important leadership principles you can honor. As a leader, it is vital that you set the temperature of the room, as well as the day, the week, the month, and the year. It's a lot of pressure and responsibility for a leader, but it is a key differentiator that sets apart home care businesses that apply the "24/7 Solution" to their operations. If you are not setting the temperature for the team – being the thermostat – but are reacting to the temperature – being the thermometer – you are, quite frankly, being a follower rather than a leader.

This is a very challenging part of leadership in the home care environment. Choosing not to be swayed by the temperature of the room is very challenging when your scheduler cries out in frustration, "She called out because her dog is sick, and her shift starts in fifteen minutes!" Or a team member returns from a consultation for services with a family and explains that it didn't close because they expected Medicare to cover 24/7 care. Or your team member contacts a long-time caregiver for a random drug screen, and it sets them off because they feel they're being accused of breaking the law, as opposed to recognizing it is normal protocol. These are all matters your team may face, and, as the leader, you must be the thermostat that cools down the room. In all these examples, you are one degree removed, which can often make it a bit easier to regulate.

Keeping your team at a healthy temperature is much more challenging when you are being directly addressed. Did you get accused of a wrongful termination? Did your caregiver let a client fall, and now the client is in the hospital with a brain bleed? Did a skilled facility staff member report that your seventy-year-old caregiver hit a senior? All of these scenarios are possible to encounter during your work day, and, worse yet, every single one of them can happen in a day's work. Yet you're supposed to be able to keep it together? Whew.

I get it. However, no matter how pretty or ugly the day may be, you still must be the thermostat. Keep in mind that being a thermostat doesn't mean you are not in touch with reality, or that you shouldn't communicate the reality of the situation with stakeholders. Some things require discretion and may only need to be communicated to your top leaders or those involved so that panic doesn't ensue. Every thermostat you see has two different temperatures listed: one tells you the present temperature of the room, and the other tells you the temperature the cooling/heating unit has a goal of hitting.

As a leader, you do not want to dismiss the first evaluation, the present temperature of the room. If you completely dismiss the team member's call out while only giving fifteen minutes' notice, or the wasted meeting with a family because the caller wasn't screened thoroughly to understand 24/7 care isn't covered entirely by Medicare, or the irate caregiver who feels their integrity was being questioned, you are bound to upset your team, and you are more likely to have a difficult time bringing the temperature of the room back to the goal. You have to accept the reality – the current temperature of the room – name it, and then, with your team, decide how you are going to effect change.

Mission Joy

One of my favorite audiobooks is *The Book of Joy: Lasting Happiness in a Changing World*. In this book, Archbishop Desmond Tutu and the Dalai Lama are interviewed by Douglas Abrams about a variety of subjects, all of which tie back to the joy both Archbishop Desmond Tutu and the Dalai Lama seem to constantly carry with ease. The book consists of a transcript of this interview, and the audiobook is the recording itself. During this interview, you hear these two long-time friends from very different spiritual backgrounds discuss their approach to joy.

In 2021, this book was converted into a documentary and aired on Netflix as *Mission: Joy - Finding Happiness in Troubled Times*. This documentary goes beyond the interview and shares a story from professor of psychology and psychiatry Dr. Richard Davidson. In 1992, the Dalai Lama asked Dr. Davidson to study the mind of Tibetan monks who had spent years training their mind. He was challenged by the Dalai Lama to use the same tools he was using to study depression, anxiety, and fear to study kindness and compassion instead.

They conducted an experiment in which individuals were exposed to incredibly hot water that caused immediate pain while under MRI evaluation. In addition, they were given a tone to associate with this pain (hot water), and a different tone was associated with no pain (warm water). They evaluated individuals that had never meditated and compared them to the Tibetan monks. When the tone associated with pain was played to the group who spent time training their minds via mediation, nothing would happen in the pain circuits of their brains. At least, not until the actual hot water was applied a few seconds later. At that time, the pain circuits would be activated. On the other hand, those who had never spent time training their mind would hear the tone and, immediately, their pain circuits would light up, in anticipation of the pain.

Even more fascinating is that those individuals who had not trained their mind via meditation continued to have their pain circuits lit for many moments following the removal of pain. The Tibetan monks' pain circuits lit up *only* when the heat was being applied.

What does this exercise tell us? In *Mission: Joy*, Dr. Richardson makes a simple but very radical conclusion: "well-being is a skill." He goes on to explain that when human beings first began to evolve on this planet, none of us would brush our teeth daily, yet, today, most of the people on earth do so. Why don't we consider practices like meditation to support well-being as necessary parts of improving our mental health, the same way we know brushing our teeth is necessary to maintain our physical health?

In the home care world, this study's results tell us that if we practice being in control of our mind, we can avoid having anxiety over what may or may not happen, be fully in the present, react to pain only in the moment it occurs, and move forward without ruminating on past harm. For example:

Anxiety	Presence	Solutions	Rumination
Expect a call out/ no call, no show.	Match shifts ongoing until a caregiver tells you otherwise and get ahead on shifts.	Develop a system to respond to last minute call outs more quickly.	Vent to your spouse that you had three call outs two days ago.
Expect not to close a new client.	Provide a service to the senior in need and solve their problems where possible.	Conduct regular training with team members and role-play closing clients.	Worry that your business doesn't bring value.
Expect a caregiver to make a bad impression.	Provide a caregiver with all the tools possible to make them a success.	Develop clear assessments to be followed, create trainings to convey the importance of assessments, introduce caregivers for their first shift with a client, etc.	Be embarrassed that a caregiver screwed up.
Expect a new team member to quit.	Provide a team member with all the tools possible to help them stay on and show committed support daily.	Develop a robust onboarding plan, conduct check-ins on satisfaction, be slow to hire versus responding desperately, cross train fellow employees so you do not have to hire out of desperation, etc.	Walk on eggshells, worried they will quit.
Expect team members to push back against accountability.	Put the needs of the business first and ensure you do not act to cause direct harm. Accept everyone's reactions at face value.	Develop systems of accountability *with* your team members instead of dictating them to your team; create a measure of success for any new projects and express those expectations on the front end.	Be concerned you hurt someone's feelings and they didn't say anything.

2

WHO, WHAT, WHEN, WHERE, WHY, AND THEN HOW?

To begin running a successful home care business, you need to have the answers to the following questions: *who, what, when, where,* and *why.* Not only do you, as the owner, need to know these answers, but every team member also needs to know the answers. All of this has to be clear before you can excel in the *how.* To some of you, this is basic; others may still be debating whether to provide care on the weekends, or whether to provide shifts where a caregiver sleeps at the client's place overnight.

No matter your situation, here is a basic look at the answers. Let's take them in order.

Who	Seniors and senior care professionals.
What	Provide services to seniors, for example: ADLs, IADLs.
When	Based on the senior's needs.
Where	Primarily where the senior calls home.
Why	Let's discuss.

In his book *Start With Why,* Simon Sinek speaks on the concept of the Golden Circle. At the center of that circle is *why,* next is *how,* and following that is *what.* Over the course of his book, Sinek provides examples time and time again of business leaders who turned around existing businesses or started incredibly successful businesses all because of their core understanding that their *why* is at the center of all that they do. Sinek proved the power of having a mission-driven culture.

Golden Circle

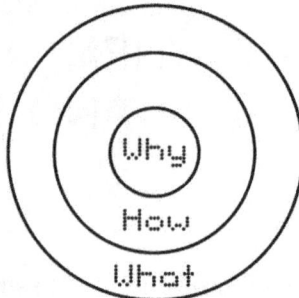

We will continue to discuss the importance of having *why* at the center of everything you do; it is a key component in running a successful home care business. We'll also hit on a common mistake home care business leaders make when it comes to communicating their *why* and utilizing it in leadership, business development, and service to seniors.

In 2012, at a time when Best Buy was struggling to keep their stores open, Hubert Joly became its CEO. Because of Joly's stubborn and confident mindset focused on a "mission-driven culture," he was able to turn the business around drastically and eventually squash the competition. Time and time again, there are examples where a "mission-driven culture" leader steps into an organization and improves revenues *and* profits. What you don't hear about is the time these leaders spend swimming upstream, bringing the stakeholders on board with their *why*, then getting stakeholders to thread the company's *why* throughout the culture and day-to-day operations. Creating a culture around a mission takes much more than writing a mission statement and putting it on your website, documents, and even a plaque on the wall.

The good news? The home care industry makes the mission part easy. I haven't met a home care business owner, senior care industry vendor, caregiver, senior, or administrative team member who doesn't have a personal story as to why they work in or near the home care industry. Finding your *why* or your team's *why* isn't hard.

On March 14, 2012, one of the last Britannica door-to-door salesmen, Myron Taxman, was given the news that the encyclopedia he had been selling for twenty-eight years was no longer going to be printed. After 244 years, the Encyclopedia Britannica was going digital. There is no doubt he had a *why* that kept him going until his very last day. Mr. Taxman believed in the product he was selling, even if everyone else believed in moving digital. It can be assumed that his *why* was his belief in the power of holding a book in your hand. Thank goodness we are not Mr. Taxman, selling something that is on the verge of becoming obsolete. Instead, we are in the perfect spot to serve an industry that is going to continue to be needed; even better, the silver tsunami is just getting to the shore.

In the early 2000s, home care owners predicted that, within the next twenty years, robots would be providing home care and were mildly afraid of this threat. Those twenty years have come and gone, and, while we are finding ways to build technology for the home to meet the demands of senior care, the robots of today are nowhere near the state or level of sophistication needed to provide this service. What is true for the foreseeable future is that technology cannot replace the quality of care a one-on-one caregiver provides. What is also true is that the number of caregivers able to provide this care will not match the demand.

So, why do you do this? Why are you a home care business owner?

For me, when I started in 2007, I was awestruck by the idea that you could be paid to provide care to a senior. I grew up in a rural area. This meant I didn't play in a cul-de-sac with neighborhood kids and had to find creative ways to socialize. It wasn't long into my adolescence that I found companionship through paying visits to my neighbor, Bessy. She was a petite woman with coal-black, curly hair who lived in a tiny, solid cobalt blue camper about 200 yards away from my house. In exchange for helping with a handful of chores my youthful legs could withstand, Bessy crushed and saved her Sprite cans for me to recycle. At a very young age, I quickly developed a heart for feeble hands and wise words.

Over time, Bessy became less and less independent, and eventually moved into a nursing home before I had a chance to say goodbye. The idea of being paid in exchange for my help never crossed my mind. The Sprite cans were a gift, not a currency. In 2007, when I learned you could earn a living while serving a senior in need, I centered my *why* around caregiving as a profession and service. I began spreading the word to families, medical healthcare providers, and hourly workers alike.

By 2012, my *why* evolved. More people were becoming familiar with the home care industry and, unfortunately, more people were experiencing poor services. By this time, I was overseeing an office in Franklin, Tennessee – a suburb of Nashville. I met regularly with family members who had terminated their relationship with one of our competitors. Story after story, I would hear about service providers failing repeatedly to make right with a client after an unfortunate incident with a caregiver, and, more often than not, failing to provide a reliable, trustworthy service. I was always careful to recognize that there are three sides to every story, as they say: yours, mine, and the truth. However, after enough time hearing these stories and watching these families experience our care, it was evident that we provided service with integrity.

We all have had "that" client or "that" daughter; those existed for us, too. But the number of, dare I say, "horror stories" of theft, abuse, and failure to answer the business phone were astounding. When these clients joined our services, they were relieved, and were rarely "that" client or "that" daughter. The *why* I now centered myself on and what I told my team regularly was that we needed to be the provider *before* someone experienced poor home care services and decided against home care altogether.

By the end of 2019, when I was finding myself less involved with visiting families and working directly with caregivers, my personal *why* evolved to building leaders who would impact the senior care industry for years to come.

Your *why* can evolve over time. Do you remember what your *why* used to be? Is it time to find a new *why*? Is that ugly "B-word" constantly boiling up in your mind? You know the one – burnout. If so, it may be time to pause and reset your *why*. It is okay if it has changed since opening day. What isn't okay is if you are not recognizing your failure to connect with the old *why* and going through the motions without a *why* today.

So, I ask again, but with an emphasis on who you are today. *Why* do you do this? *Why* are you a home care business owner?

3

KEY COMPONENTS OF A WHY-CENTERED CULTURE

You've likely heard the term "mission-driven culture." This is definitely a culture worth aspiring to, though I believe there is a more holistic culture to seek. Inspired by Sinek's Golden Circle, I led and later coined the concept of a "why-centered" team culture. A "why-centered culture" goes beyond the company's mission, is driven by why you do what you do, but has a handful of other key components that keep the company, ownership, and leadership in check.

Mission Statement

If you are a franchise owner, the franchise has likely provided you with the mission for the company. If not, or you're an independent home care owner, take a moment to utilize the *Why-Centered* tool my website provides to develop your home care business' mission. I mentioned before that it is crucial to answer the questions *who, what, when, where,* and *why* before you can determine how you'll do it. While the *what* is summed up as services, such as providing ADL and IADLs to the *who,* seniors, I often say your mission statement is also what you do. If your mission statement is "to be the most responsive service provider to seniors," then that is what you do and what you plan to do for your community. This is a wonderful mission. However, to ensure a fully "why-centered culture," you need to enact your *why.*

A common mistake in the home care industry is believing that your mission statement is enough, or that it actually does enact your *why*. When providers fall prey to this, they use their mission statement in every document signed by employees, on their website, and throughout their marketing material without realizing they are only staying focused on the outer edges of the Golden Circle, the *what*.

Golden Circle

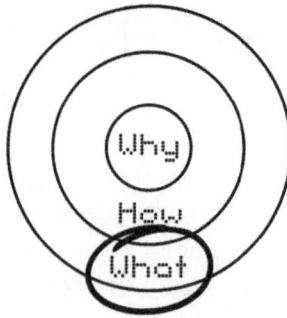

To help us get to the core we need to go deeper than a mission statement. That is where the *core purpose* comes into play.

Core Purpose

To develop a fully "why-centered culture," you need to finalize a core purpose. This purpose, coupled with the mission statement, provides full clarity to your stakeholders as to why you show up to work every day and why your organization exists. Perhaps your core purpose is "to relentlessly pursue every avenue to provide seniors with independence in their home." Coupling this with the mission statement from before, your stakeholders would know that you are the most responsive service provider to seniors and you will relentlessly pursue every avenue to provide seniors independence at home.

Said another way, you're going to show up in a pinch no matter what it takes to make sure seniors stay home. A daughter is going to know that you will not only be responsive to her needs, but that your goals also align with her goal to keep her mother home. Your company's *why* mirrors the daughter's *why*, and trust is built. Additionally, a potential employee who had a similar experience to the one I had with my neighbor, Bessy, may recognize that your company can help future Bessys live out their last days in their home.

Both the mission statement and core purpose are key in providing quality service and exceptional leadership within your company. However, there is one key foundational piece still missing to develop a fully "why-centered culture" – a set of core values.

Core Values

Without core values, your business will have an expiration date. There will come a point where you will be driven by your mission and core purpose so strongly that you fail to consider the harm you may cause to stakeholders along the way. Core values provide you with guardrails that keep you and your business honest. Some companies have more than twenty core values. I personally recommend four to six succinct values. Having fewer values ensures that your team can get to know them inside and out. Similarly, it allows you as the owner to know and embody them consistently. The more these are embedded into your culture, the better.

A well-known company that exudes a "why-centered culture" and keeps mission, purpose, and values top of mind is Southwest Airlines. One of their core values is "win the right way."

Let's imagine a scenario with the example mission statement and core purpose from before, and a core value of "win the right way," like Southwest.

Mission: *To be the most responsive service provider to seniors.*

Core Purpose: *To relentlessly pursue every avenue to provide seniors with independence in their home.*

One Core Value: *Win the right way.*

With these three "why-centered" principles in place, a provider is much less likely to do whatever it takes at the expense of an employee.

Core values ensure you do what is right, not just what is easy.

Instead of saying, "I don't care if she worked the past twenty-four hours, we need her to go to this shift!" the leader and the administrative team member are much more likely to say, "how can we find another way to ensure this senior gets responsive care and this caregiver is able to rest?" Core values ensure you do what is right, not just what is easy.

I regularly reference a hunter-gatherer mindset with business leaders. While it was millennia ago that we lived in a hunter-gatherer world, we still have instincts tied deeply to this mindset. As our world has become more industrialized, we have gone further and further away from being able to scratch this innate itch. Ever since the ability to safely store food became the norm and not a luxury, our society has moved away from being concerned about making our next kill or when we need to go out and gather fruit, herbs, and roots – at least, in the literal sense. It is still very much a reality that people and families are concerned about their ability to put food on the table.

I'm going to assume that a majority of your administrative team members are not waking up every day only to set about trying to find their next meal. As a result, their equivalent of hunting and gathering today is less tied to the immediate reward of a meal. Because it helps me to think in pictures, I've provided a handful of graphics. The first graphic illustrates our roots.

The Hunter-Gatherer Cycle

Once a week, every two weeks, or twice a month, your team members earn a paycheck for showing up to work. The multiple twenty-four-hour days between their work and their paycheck creates an incredible disconnect in their psychology. This disconnect is represented by the lighter gray arrow between work and money below.

Modern Hunter-Gatherer Cycle

As leaders, it is our role to remind our team members of the reward they are receiving from their work. Amidst challenges and celebrations, we need to bridge the gap between effort and reward, and we definitely need to do this without saying "that's why you get a paycheck" on repeat. So, how can we bridge the disconnect within their psychology from work to reward?

One of the first and easiest ways to do this is to thread our mission statement and core purpose throughout everything that we do. If we want sustainable careers for ourselves and our caregivers, we have to amplify the rewards given during the span of time between your team member doing the work and them receiving their paycheck for that work. Beyond the leadership of your team and the probability that they will carry your message into their day-to-day work lives, your team members' home care careers will be more sustainable. What can you do as a leader today that would better illustrate the rewards of what we do every day in the life of a caregiver?

The Home Care Hunter-Gatherer Cycle

We will continue to talk more about this concept throughout the book, but the hunter-gatherer cycle and your leadership in tying your team back to the mission and core purpose are key differentiators between a successful home care business and one that is running on fumes.

Be sure to take a moment to truly identify your mission, core purpose, and core values by utilizing the *Why-Centered* tool at www. the247solution.com.

24/7 SOLUTION TIME

Keep in mind, the "why-centered culture" is a holistic take on being a mission-minded culture. Putting the mission of your company top of mind for you and your team is important, but only a portion of what it takes to embed a culture that is truly devoted to living out that mission and doing so with integrity.

Now that we have answered the questions, *who, what, when, where,* and *why* and tied them to a "why-centered culture," we are finally ready to dive into answering the *how.* The rest of this book will speak to how you can run a successful home care business. I often say when providing keynotes that, to provide you a complete guide on *how,* you would need to earn a doctorate degree in home care. I may be exaggerating a bit, but my point is that these next pages provide the foundational steps of *how.* Within each *how,* there are layers that go deeper and deeper into the best ways to execute your organization's operations well.

My hope for you is that the self-leadership principles addressed in a previous chapter, along with the foundational steps that you are about to learn, will lead to your ability to continue to evolve and improve on your business' operations successfully for years to come. Every one of my clients knows that when they work with me, our services have an end date. My goal is to work with as many home care providers in the industry as possible. My *why* is to help both seniors and senior care workers thrive in a white-glove approach to care across the globe. We can only do this by setting each client up to be self-sufficient. This book is designed with the same goal in mind. The idea is that you will develop a concrete approach to your business that your own self-leadership can evolve for years to come.

4

ROLES AND RESPONSIBILITIES

Last chapter, we discussed the hunter-gatherer cycle of work to reward. This chapter, we are going to take that analogy further and discuss the "food" your team is hunting or gathering for the "meal" each day. Understanding this is the next key differentiator that will lead to a successful home care business.

There are a handful of "24/7 Solution Time" sections within this chapter meant to indicate stopping spots. I recommend honoring each of these stops. I also strongly recommend you do not announce any changes to your organization until you have fully completed each "24/7 Solution Time" stop in this chapter. Having a full picture of your organization's roles and responsibilities in combination with your finances is necessary before you can implement next steps.

I often say to my clients: **Positions before people or profit**. Off the cuff, this sounds a bit odd. Why would anything ever come before profit? And aren't positions, in effect, people? This phrase is designed to make you think.

The most common mistake I find clients making is that they misalign roles and responsibilities. Oftentimes, their decisions on the jobs people are doing have been swayed by the personalities of the people doing those jobs. We're going to discuss more about what I mean by that, but, first, we need to conduct an evaluation of your administrative team.

To conduct this evaluation, please go to my website to download the *Channels Exercise*. During this exercise, you will be assigning your team members' tasks to different channels. Once it is complete, you will be able to determine whether you have prioritized *positions before people and profit* appropriately.

Now that you have downloaded the *Channels Exercise*, you will need to get a clear picture of what your team does daily. As I mentioned before, what is it that each team member is bringing to the "meal" each day? There are two ways to measure this. When you download the *Channels Exercise*, it comes with a few additional tools, specifically the *Time Journal* and *Time Exercise Questionnaire*. I do not recommend using both; I would simply pick the one that is most conducive to your leadership style, your team's bandwidth, and the one that makes the most sense to you.

Once you receive each team member's answers, including your own, place the data into the *Task List* document and follow the instructions carefully. One of the most important instructions to be mindful of is making sure you color code each team member and their corresponding tasks with their own designated color. Once you have completed this, you will then want to refer to the tool titled *Roles and Responsibility Guide* to compare your results.

24/7 SOLUTION TIME

If your breakdown shows one color is falling in a single column, and the column matches the department they are working in – great! Your foundation is ready to build upon. If your breakdown looks more like a Jackson Pollock painting, with splotches of color every-where, there's no need to panic, but this is likely a key part of the reason why your business is not exactly where you want it to be. While it is not always true for everyone that completes this exercise, it is common that the reason the color of the channels are not clean is because an owner is putting *people* before *positions*.

Since 2007, I have noticed that a lot of home care owners will shoot from the hip when it comes to developing positions in their business. Rather than starting with an *Organizational Chart of the Future*, they create positions based on the directions they are being pulled. Sometimes this pulling occurs due to their own weaknesses, and sometimes as a result of their team member's strengths. If we all had our preference, we would do what we *want* to do, not what we *need* to do. This constant friction without standards and expectations to hold it accountable causes businesses to suffer.

If we all had our preference, we would do what we *want* to do, not what we *need* to do.

So often, I hear from clients: "Susie is really wonderful with clients. She handles all caregiver hiring and training and, since she is incredible with our clients, we trained her to do sales calls in the home with potential clients."

"John is really great with caregivers, so when he isn't doing marketing and sales, we have him help staff shifts. He is such a great salesperson, hardly any caregiver ever tells him 'no' when he calls to ask them to work a shift. We call him our secret weapon!"

Potentially even more damaging to the business results, I've even had owners who love caregiver education so much that they insist on hosting weekly orientation themselves, tying up one to two days a week in their schedule as a result.

People **before** positions or profits.

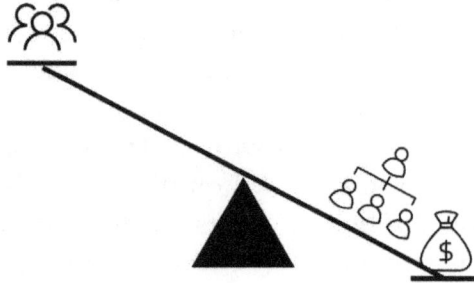

This reactive, personality-based approach is always well-intended. Owners want to ensure that nothing gets missed, that team members' positions play to their strengths, and that everyone is happy. However, as we think back to the *Channels Exercise*, what is really happening is that too many people are doing the same job and there are a lot of different colors in one channel. The owner is throwing splotches of color in different channels in hopes of ensuring the aforementioned three things.

Roles & Responsibility Channels

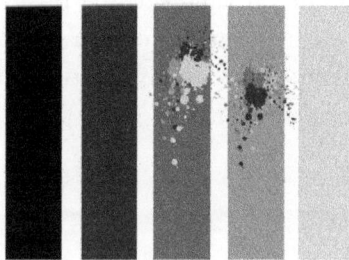

Potentially even more problematic is that, while the owner is throwing color into other channels, she's failing to keep other tasks covered. This means that other tasks are not being accomplished. While this may be okay as a response to a snow day or some sort of natural disaster, this cannot be the daily approach to running a business.

Roles & Responsibility
Channels

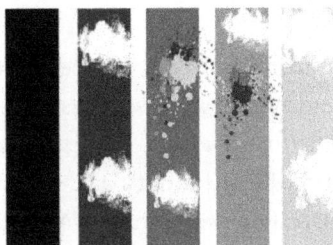

As you can see from the *Channels Exercise* you downloaded, there are six channels a home care business needs to fill: five departments, plus an owner/operator role. Everything can fall into one of the five departments. Those departments, in no particular order, are:

1. Human Resources – all things caregiver-facing only.
2. Quality Assurance – all things client-facing only.
3. Scheduling – schedules pertaining to both clients and caregivers.
4. Marketing – all things necessary for new client acquisition.
5. Finance – accounts receivable, accounts payable, payroll.

From this starting point, you can begin to define roles and responsibilities for your organization. If you have a clinical arm in your business, you may benefit from identifying your Quality Assurance department as Nursing or Clinical instead, although, depending on your state's requirements, it may be financially beneficial to place a registered nurse under Quality Assurance. In other words, you can place a Quality Assurance leader who oversees an RN. There are some key factors to consider before making a decision to this end, such as the cost of an RN on staff, the demand of clinical needs your clients may have throughout the lifetime of your services, and whether this position can be contracted.

The revenue your organization carries consistently is the best and safest determinant for the organization's needs. It is healthy to keep an administrative percentage of 13% or less in your business; ideally, it should be closer to 11-12%. I do not recommend skimping and trying to save money here. Less than 11% is very risky and is an example of putting profits before positions or people. Remember, *positions before people or profit.*

To calculate your administrative percentage, simply review the dollars spent on your administrative salaries in a month and compare this to your gross monthly revenue. For easy math, if you pay your administrative team $100.00 in January and bill your clients $1,000.00 in January; your administrative percentage was $100.00/$1,000, or 10%. In home care, you will always have up and down trends. Some months have more days than others, and, every leap year, we get an extra day of revenue. Given the fluidity of this reality, it is important to look at a few months of historical data as you make decisions about your business.

Now that we know the cost breakdown, we can determine how many positions your business can likely afford. Keep in mind, the smaller your organization and the more expensive the cost of living for your territory, the fewer positions you will be able to have before increasing your client's rates or finding other avenues to earn revenue. With fewer positions being financially feasible, and able to be filled, the owner/operator is going to have to wear more hats. This idea is never popular, but when executed properly, you will be earning incredible profits and growing your organization so quickly that the temporary inconvenience will quickly be forgotten. With all of this in mind, it is also vitally important to save on overhead. Do you really need brand new furniture for everyone's office?

Whether you are a fan of Jeff Bezos, envious, or indifferent, he did a lot of things right on his way to becoming the billionaire he is today. When he began his company, every desk was made from *doors.* The story goes that their first office was across the street from a Home Depot. As Bezos looked at the price of a desk versus a door, he couldn't ignore the savings a door would bring if he just put some legs on it. Years later, many of his employees worldwide still work each day at a door desk. Furthermore, Bezos' scrappy mindset of getting more with less became part of the culture that still exists today. Talk about a "why-centered culture." These door desks represent the idea that we don't need to overcomplicate functionality, and furthermore, they represent ingenuity and creativity. All are key parts of what made Bezos' organization the success it is today.

As an organization that needs to present professionally to future caregivers and potential clients, perhaps the door desk isn't a solution. However, a "24/7 Solution" to saving money might be finding used desks online that will serve your office well. During my entire time building organizations, I never sat at a brand new desk, yet we always presented ourselves very professionally.

Back to the *Organizational Chart of the Future* (moving forward, we will call it *Org Chart of the Future*) and how to ensure you are putting *positions before people or profit*. Visit my website for a breakdown of the *Org Chart of the Future* you can use to help you make plans for your business as you grow revenues. Losing sight of this plan is what leads owners to put *people or profit* **before** *positions*. As you think about *positions before people or profits*, be mindful not to choose a door desk when you need a desk with drawers. What I mean by this is, do not skimp on positions and try to get by with cheap solutions. Choosing *profit before people or positions* can happen in the planning stage, months or years before the decision to hire arrives. As you plan this out, always remember that choosing profits before positions or people is not sustainable and will lead your profits to suffer long term.

Profits **before** positions or people.

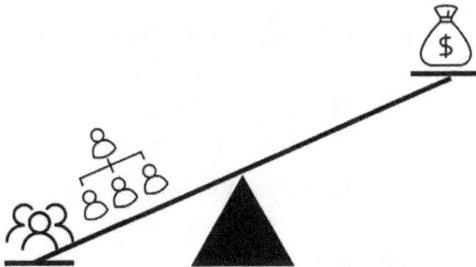

Although this scale appears exciting at first glance, it is important to remember those profits are very, *very* temporary.

Next, take time to evaluate the *Org Chart of the Future* tool for your organization. Be patient with yourself, allow yourself to sleep on the decisions you make, and revisit them a few times before confirming faith in this process. As you do this exercise, it is important to truly create forecasts for many future phases of the business. Why? There are a few reasons, but an especially common challenge I have encountered with owners is that they have team members on staff who cannot help the owners take their business to the next level. Even the best planning will not fully prevent this from happening in your business, but I have to imagine if you start with the end in mind, your trajectory can be a little less bumpy. If you are continuing to recruit, onboard, and train your team members while keeping in mind the types of positions and people you will one day need, you are much less likely to find yourself in a place where you need to do a major overhaul because of people's limited or poorly matched skill sets.

One of my prouder moments occurred in 2014. The office where I got my start was up for an award at our annual conference: they had achieved $400,000/month in revenue, a majority of which came from private pay clients. Based on the market at the time, this averaged out to about 22,500 hours a month of care to seniors. For those readers who think in terms of weeks, this landed us around 5,500 hours of care a week from a more rural franchise territory. We were doing incredibly well, and, on top of that, out of all of the Home Instead locations, this particular office was number one in terms of market saturation. While all of that was worthy of our pride, what made me the proudest was something else altogether.

As the team of day-to-day administrative team members went on stage to receive their award, I recognized that all but one of the fifteen team members on stage had been hired as caregivers during my time in the HR Department. The only one I didn't hire as a caregiver was an individual who was in the office longer than I had been with the company. Because the owner of the company had done such an incredible job with their vision for the future roles our organization would need, I was able to vet caregivers for potential administrative opportunities and begin discussing their career paths with them right away. It still pains me today when I hear someone say, "We tried hiring caregivers; it just doesn't work for us." We'll discuss this more later, but the point of this chapter is that having a clear understanding of the positions you need before meeting the people that may fill them or cutting corners for profits that sacrifice the value of each role is one of the most important items in your business to hold in balance.

Positions before people or profits.

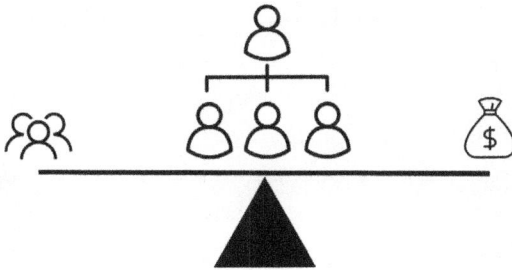

Now, it is time for you to complete the *Channels Exercise* to evaluate how you will begin to manage your organization's current and immediate needs.

24/7 SOLUTION TIME

Job Descriptions

Now that you have outlined your *Org Chart of the Future*, it is time to determine the details of the job descriptions for each position. A sample job description can be found on *The 24/7 Solution* website. One mistake people commonly make when crafting a job description is making it too detailed. There is a particular sweet spot you need to fall within when developing a job description. You want the candidate to have a general idea of what a day or week in the life of someone in the position looks like, but you do not want it to be so detailed that it screams "that's a lot of work." In addition to being just enough, you will want to make sure the job description is as timeless as possible.

How can you make information timeless? Getting hyperspecific with details such as the brand of telephony used to manage caregiver arrival times, or using descriptions like "must review this system daily and ensure caregivers are clocked in and out by logging it in x software," make a job description less timeless. For example, you would want to avoid describing a duty with, "log into ABC Telephony Systems every day to ensure notifications are managed and any discrepancies are placed into XYZ Scheduler Toolz." Technology is always changing quickly, so a better alternative may be, "utilize and manage technology software to ensure caregivers are arriving timely to provide seniors with dependable trustworthy care." A potential team member will read the latter and immediately tell that dependable, trustworthy care is an important value for this company. On the other hand, if they read the former, they may get completely lost in the weeds, and, in reading branded names, they may assume they are expected to already know those systems before applying.

In addition, using this broader language allows the technology platforms you use to be irrelevant. If your company converts to a different platform in six months, you do not have to concern yourself with updating the job description and getting an updated signature from your team members. As you read this, you may be scoffing at the idea of needing to get signatures to update a job description. That is why having as timeless of a job description as possible is so important. As a 24/7 business, we need to protect ourselves from extra, unnecessary work in the future. That is one of many themes of a "24/7 Solution" mindset.

There is a Farmers Insurance commercial in which it is said, "We know a thing or two because we've seen a thing or two." I can attest to one too many experiences where we had to learn this the hard way. It is commonly understood that if a dispute makes it to the court system, for example, an unemployment hearing, the judge will often lean toward showing empathy for the employee as opposed to the employer. If the employee were to bring the job description as evidence to support their case, and the signature is attached to a technology platform that is no longer being used, it is very easy for the employee to say "I was never trained on that platform and I had no way of ensuring x, y, or z. How can I be terminated for something I wasn't ever trained properly on how to do?" It has often been said, if it's not documented, it didn't happen. No matter what you know to be true, if it's not documented, it didn't happen – and it is their document against your word. Who do you think the judge is going to believe?

Lastly, a common mistake owners make with job descriptions is to try to give the exact details of the job. When describing a day in the life, your gut approach may be to provide applicants with a checklist of things that will need to be done. Instead, it is better to write the bullet points for this job description in such a way that you are speaking to the results of the work. For example, a task for an HR position might be to "conduct phone screenings," and another task may be to "conduct interviews." Listing each of these and more is giving the candidate a "day in the life" view, but it's also not likely to interest them and puts the document at risk of not being timeless. Instead, write "conduct all necessary screening of potential candidates to find the most qualified individuals to meet the ever-growing demands of our client base."

Going back to our *Channels Exercise*, it's time to create updated job descriptions. To expand upon the idea of *positions before people or profit*, we need to create job descriptions for jobs within each channel. Take a moment to look at the *Org Chart of the Future* tool on my website to get an idea of the quantity of positions you need to fill per department. The larger the monthly revenues in your business, the more demand you have for administrative team support. Keep in mind that an administrative percentage of (or less than) 13% to be put toward your office should be your true measure of how many employees your departments can have.

Prior to implementing changes based on administrative percentage alone, you must evaluate your profit margins and gross margins. If your gross margins are much lower than 45-50%, you may have a problem with how much you are paying your caregivers and how much you are charging your clients. If your profit margins are in the red every month, you may have an issue with too much overhead expense, in which case, you need to begin cleaning up areas where you have financial waste. While the 13% administrative percentage is an important figure to evaluate, it is important as the owner of your organization to recognize other financial weaknesses in your operations. If you are interested in obtaining a *Financial Scorecard Audit*, you can go to www.the247solution.com to inquire about our availability to conduct one for your organization.

Now, it is time to develop the job descriptions you need for your business based on the *Org Chart of the Future*.

24/7 SOLUTION TIME

Job Descriptions per Size

Smaller businesses with less revenue will require team members to wear more hats. However, it is still important for you to make your hiring decisions with departmental coverage in mind. We will discuss this in more detail, but one of the main disadvantages to being a new organization or to having low monthly revenues is that the owner/ operator must wear a lot of hats as well. A lot of challenges for an organization's ability to grow are caused by the owner's decision to put important tasks on the back burner or push those important tasks onto unqualified team members. The refusal by an owner to step into the day-to-day when the organization is relatively small is what will keep an organization small.

When it comes to managing scheduling, one of the main pain points for most home care owners, there tends to be two schools of thought on the best way to manage this role.

One school of thought believes that when an organization is small, there isn't a need for a full-time scheduler. When taking this mindset, a business hires an individual and gives them the primary responsibility of scheduling, but with an understanding that they will also handle anything extra. This may lead the owner/operator and the rest of the team to develop a mindset of, "Oh, Lucy, our scheduler, can help with that."

Before long, Lucy is responsible for interviews with caregivers, conducting training, completing reference checks, and handling complaints with clients or client family members. When an inquiry for a new 24/7 client calls to request care, the office communicates that it cannot begin care for two weeks because Lucy isn't ready. With a two-week delayed start, this family calls the next provider and starts care with a competitor.

Depending on your rates for care, this one decision may cost the organization $36,000/month in revenue. If you think about it, this issue occurred because the organization put *profits **before** positions or people*. They decided the details of Lucy's job based on saving money and getting more bang for their buck with her pay. But, as you can see, this decision to put savings from having fewer new hires first was incredibly short-sighted and did not create a capacity for them to grow their profits long term.

Profits **before** positions or people.

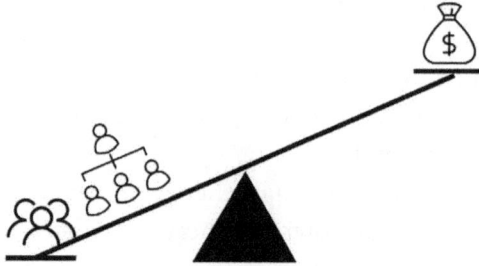

Boy, do I get the initial appeal of this school of thought.

The other school of thought is that everyone needs to leave employees in charge of scheduling alone to schedule. If they have time to scroll social media one day, so be it. Tomorrow, they may be dealing with a no call, no show and three call outs due to the flu. I am a strong advocate for this approach.

A "24/7 Solution" would not allow your scheduler ample time to scroll social media, but it would allow that scheduler to stand ready to serve a scheduling demand promptly. How can we make sure we're not wasting money on their labor costs? The first step we must take is forecasting the future of their position. They need to understand that the percentage of time they spend matching caregivers with clients will evolve as the organization grows. What I have found to be one of the best ways to keep your schedulers ready to serve immediate needs while ensuring they do not waste labor dollars is to set *trim goals*. I created this concept after finding myself frustrated watching schedulers get ahead of schedules and ending up with a lot of extra time on their hands. A *trim goal* is the understanding that, as the business grows, you will slowly trim down the goal expectations set forth.

Let's go back to the job description for a moment. The job description may contain the following: "Schedule all open assignments for clients with a compatible, ongoing caregiver match. Conduct 'just because' calls with caregivers on a regular basis to build relationships." What you'll notice in these two sentences is that they have been kept vague (and there is no mention of scrolling social media). The number of client-to-caregiver assignment matches and number of 'just because' calls are not defined. Remember that keeping this information vague helps the job description remain as timeless as possible.

Utilizing the above highlights from a job description, a trim goal involves creating an ideal target which your scheduler should aim to hit based on the place from which they're starting in their position. For example, you might approach the concept by telling them, "As it stands today, we want you to complete thirty 'just because' calls a week with caregivers, five 'just because' calls a week with clients, and five 'just because' calls a week with client family members. As the company grows, the number of 'just because' calls we want you to achieve will decrease, because we expect you to be responding to the demands of the business which will require an increase in your other duties."

Here is a chart that shows how to effectively trim the goals you set as hours of service per week increases:

Hours/Week	Just Because Totals/Week	Caregivers	Clients	Client Family Members
Up to 500	40	30	5	5
Up to 1000	30	25	2	3
Up to 1500	20	20	0	0

In this example, the scheduler needs to be told that, after 1,500 hours, a new team metric will be established, because it is assumed that once a company is billing over 1,500 hours a week, their scheduling team will likely need an addition. As a result, you'll need to revisit what is possible in relation to these goals once the Scheduling Department hires a new administrative team member.

Similarly, it is assumed that once a company is billing 1,000 hours a week of care, their administrative team will include a Quality Assurance representative. When this team member is added, "just because" calls to clients or client family members are not needed.

When to Add to Your Team

Owners often get ahead of their skis when it comes to hiring a new position. Many business trainings attempt to impress upon students the importance of recruiting and hiring before they need the support. Many teach the concepts *slow to hire, quick to fire*, or *hire slow, fire fast*.

How do you apply the *slow to hire* concept without hiring before the need is imminent? If you hire before the need arises, how does that make financial sense for the organization? In the home care world, you almost always feel like you needed to hire someone yesterday, yet rarely do you feel confident in your ability to afford the position.

Because of the push and pull that the business of home care entails, owners often hire haphazardly. They receive a sudden bump in business and feel naively confident in their new revenue projections. One thing leads to another, and the mixture of adrenaline from the exciting revenue projections combined with an overwhelmed scheduler leads to a new full-time employee. Given the circumstances, all of this appears, at face value, to be the perfect solution to meet the demand. Then, a few weeks later, the revenue projection drops dramatically because a healthy 24/7 client suddenly passes.

Not only did you lose revenue, but the employee was also onboarded hurriedly. The new employee isn't completely sure what their number one goals are when they come to work every day. To continue with our hunter-gatherer example, they don't know what they are supposed to be bringing to the meal every day. When a client loss occurs and chaos ensues, the new person may come to view the business they just joined as disorganized and messy. If the owner doesn't terminate the new hire's employment due to financial reasons, the employee is likely to look around and say "what a mess!" quit, and may even recruit the best employees to quit with them! Even worse are the situations where the owner doesn't have the courage to dismiss the new hire and they turn out to be a bad hire. Now, they are putting the organization into the red with their payroll expense *and* their execution of tasks. Owners' best intentions unfortunately can lead them to live out the saying "one step forward, two steps back."

My approach was always methodical. For starters, I always knew my next move and communicated it accordingly. I knew we had five departments to hire for as soon as the business could grow to afford all five representatives. Until the business could afford the departments to have a representative, the tasks within that department would fall to the owner/operator to complete.

When & Who to Hire

Depart-ments	Phase 1 Onset	Phase 2 First 3-6 Months Depending on Revenue	Phase 3 6-18 Months Depending on Revenue	Phase 4 12-24 Months Depending on Revenue	Phase 5 24 Plus Months Depending on Revenue
Marketing	Owner	Owner	Owner	Owner/ Employee	Employee
Scheduling	Owner	Employee	Employee	Employee	Employee
Human Resources	Owner	Owner	Employee	Employee	Employee
Quality Assurance	Owner	Owner	Owner	Owner/ Employee	Employee
Finance	Owner	Owner/ Outsource	Owner/ Outsource	Owner/ Outsource	Employee/ Outsource

*Depending on revenue is a key factor with this chart. Revenue needs to weigh more than time; a slow growing business will take longer to get to the final phase of this chart.

As seen above, my advice for owners in the early stages of their business is for them to fill in roles in Quality Assurance and Marketing as opposed to Scheduling and Human Resources. The sooner you can afford to hire in Scheduling and Human Resources, the better. The responsibilities of these roles are not easily accomplished if you are out meeting with a family to set up services. If you are not careful, your growth will bottleneck because you cannot bring a new client and a caregiver onto your roster simultaneously as the HR representative for your company. On the other hand, if you are out marketing for your company, you can rest assured that your HR team member back at the office is adding new team members to your roster.

Once you grow to the point that you can afford a new administrative hire, and are shifting from phase three to phase four, my advice is to look in the mirror and ask yourself a few questions.

1. Are you enjoying Quality Assurance?
2. Do you enjoy Marketing more?
3. Are you good at Quality Assurance, or do clients keep leaving unhappy anyway?
4. What about Marketing – have you successfully brought on new clients from referrals?
5. Is all the new business due to digital marketing from your franchisor?

Be honest with yourself and then choose to hire for the role that the data shows is handicapping the business the most.

If you find more joy in Quality Assurance because you like visiting families, but you brought in three referrals last week from your marketing efforts, then you may need to hire for Quality Assurance regardless of where things fall on your joy meter. Here's the thing: this is all temporary, anyway.

I often say *data over dopamine*. Dopamine hits feel incredible; joy and pleasure do not need to be ignored. However, if the data is telling you that you would serve the organization better through marketing and bringing in new business right now, then put off the dopamine hits until later. I promise you, when you grow your business exponentially, you will have many more hits of dopamine in your system!

When it comes to Finance, you will still want to keep a pulse on your business' results. If you outsource, be sure to outsource bookkeeping to a bookkeeper. If your accountant is handling your bookkeeping, you are paying way too much for that service. Find a trustworthy bookkeeper and set up guardrails that ensure you have a clear idea of your business' financial picture. If you outsource to a bookkeeper and only hear from them sparingly, you may have a lazy bookkeeper. A quality bookkeeper will update you on the status of your business and ask questions throughout the month to make sure they are processing your books to your preference.

It is advisable in the early stages of your business to keep expenses minimal. This includes the hiring of an operational manager. It is not recommended to step away from your business or even put someone else in charge of operations until you are much more established. However, as an entrepreneur, it is your sole decision (assuming your franchisor allows for absentee ownership). Keep in mind that every dollar you are paying them (in the black or red) is a dollar you are not paying yourself or putting towards your debts. If you make good decisions in this phase of your business, you will be able to afford an operational manager and get paid sooner. The trick is to be patient and to not be afraid to do some of the heavy lifting on the front end.

One of the many questions I get from owners as they look at the *Org Chart of the Future* and consider the balance of keeping their administrative percentage down is, "How much were you making during the early phases?" The answer is always the same: "Enough." The mindset you need to have at this stage of the business is not served by fantasizing about buying a new boat, giving large amounts to charity, or taking that trip to Europe – you need to be focused on building a foundation. Once that foundation is built, then all of the above can occur – and, even better, you can decide on a Thursday to book a flight and a trip to Aruba for the weekend if that sounds fun! But, right now, when you're building a foundation you just need to earn "enough."

"Enough" is defined as putting food on the table, having a roof over your head, keeping the lights on, and paying down debts. Anything less than that needs to be very temporary and you need to act quickly on your business' results to ensure otherwise. Anything more than that should be saved in the business for three to six months of payroll coverage. Once those financial goals are met and the business has what it needs, you can begin paying yourself more than "enough."

Now it is time to establish the exact position your business is in today based on your administrative percentages, profits, and your skill-set as the owner.

24/7 SOLUTION TIME

5

POLICIES AND PROCEDURES

Now that we've discussed and determined the *who, what, when, where, why*, we're now ready to begin answering *how*.

If we go back to the mission statement example from Chapter 3 – "to be the most responsive service provider to seniors" – and remember that this helps answer the question of what we do, we can recognize a lot of ways we can go about accomplishing this mission. How we get there is ultimately our decision to make as the leader of our organization. The best place to start when defining how you want your organization to achieve this mission is through designing and implementing policies and procedures.

Underneath the umbrella of policies and procedures, I direct my clients to focus on *five* main resources that keep team members' eyes on the mission. Those five resources are: handbooks, operation manuals, acknowledgement forms, training sign-offs, and training agendas. All five play an equally important role in ensuring team members feel successful in their journeys with your company. The most important time frame for your employees is during their initial thirty to ninety days at your business.

Right now, we'll focus on administrative team members as opposed to caregivers. To provide the most successful onboarding experience, your employees' first thirty to sixty days need to be outlined in a well laid out training agenda. This time period is when your employee is the most coachable and energetic, and it is also the time when many of their future work habits are established. When turnover happens, it can sting, but I always took the opportunity with a new team member to improve the habits of the previous one. Sometimes, this meant replacing an "A" player with an "A-plus" performing employee. At the very least, that was always the goal.

In order to onboard well, the team members need to feel like you have a plan for them – and that you have clear expectations of them. You cannot build a habit of eating well if you don't first create a plan for doing so. In the same way, you cannot build a habit of being responsive if you don't come up with actionable steps through which you can become the most responsive service provider. In between the habit and the goal are the steps needed to ensure the desired outcome is achieved. For weight loss, you may hire a personal trainer, and that personal trainer may establish a training plan and a meal logging process. In home care, you begin by developing policies and procedures.

Handbooks

The best place to start is by developing a handbook. The handbook is where the rules of employment are kept. I recommend a handbook for your administrative team and a similar, though separate, one for your caregivers. Prioritize creating one for your caregivers, because a large percentage of the items in the caregiver handbook may apply to your administrative handbook as well. If nothing else, the caregiver handbook can easily be adapted into an administrative handbook and you can use the caregiver one as the agreed-upon rules until you're able to make the administrative handbook.

What are some common rules of employment that should be addressed? Items like your policy against workplace harassment, your drug and alcohol policy, the dress code, and – especially crucial in the home care industry – your rules about confidentiality. In addition to rules of employment, the handbook is a good place to record information about benefits. If someone is trying to remember when their vacation benefit begins or whether they qualify as a part-time employee, the handbook needs to answer their questions. My website provides a list of what could be included in your company's handbook to make sure you're not missing any important information.

In addition to addressing these bare minimum needs, handbooks provide another place to set the stage for your mission. Starting the handbook with an overview of the mission, core values, and core purpose of your organization is a great way to remind your team members *why* they show up for work every day. You can even make the handbook interactive and add a fill in the blank spot for them to answer their *why*. This little touch may serve to help in grounding your team members whenever they get upset about being held accountable to a policy in the handbook.

Imagine this: four months into your team member's time with the company, they are held accountable for being tardy and they become upset. In their anger, they are confident that they were never told that "x" amount of tardies would lead to a written counseling. As such, they dive into their handbook, flip to the table of contents, and come across a page with their handwriting stating why they come to work every day. They pause and, suddenly, are taken back to their first week with the company, back to their excitement to be joining such a powerful mission, so much so that they almost forget why they got their handbook out in the first place. As they remember and look at their *why*, they scan the page they are on and are reminded that the company's mission is to be the most responsive service provider. Suddenly, they realize that their tardiness (regardless of why they were tardy) does not represent the company's mission. Sure, they may have huffed at their supervisor for the counseling, but this handbook just provided this team member with the tools to hold themselves accountable.

The handbook is your go-to resource for employees to find the answers to most of their employment relationship questions. Include a table of contents, and work with legal counsel to make sure that you are fully compliant with all local and federal labor laws.

Some businesses choose to have their employees sign multiple forms – such as getting a signature from them that they understand the dress code, or a signature denoting their understanding of disciplinary action. This is definitely better than not having anything; however, this leaves the employee without a copy of what they signed. Once they are out in the field and have questions about the policies to which they agreed, they may not have a copy for reference. A handbook with all of this information and a single acknowledgement form signed can save the employee from hand cramps, your files from getting weighed down with paper, and, if you are actually printing everything versus keeping electronic files, a few trees can let out some breaths of relief.

When working on the handbook, you want most of the information listed to be as timeless as possible – "timeless" meaning that you hope you do not have to edit or change the content for months to come, if not years. This doesn't mean you avoid edits; it just means you should write it in such a way that changes won't be necessary. Changing the handbook frequently will create issues and is also time-consuming. Again, don't avoid doing it if it *is* necessary. The desire to create as timeless as possible reference materials is a necessary "24/7 Solution" mentality when it comes to growing and scaling your home care organization.

Now, it is time to create your handbook – or edit your existing handbook – based on the guidelines described.

24/7 SOLUTION TIME

Operation Manuals

If all you have in place is a handbook, then you are better off than some, but still greatly behind many others. An employee understanding their relationship with their employer is very important. Once you have this done, it's important to help your employees understand how to perform their jobs in the organization; this "how-to" is where a manual comes into play. I like to make the distinction between the two in this way: A handbook will guide you on how to do well *as an employee*, while a manual will guide you on how to do well *in your job*.

You can add this information to the caregiver handbook directly, but for administrative team members, it is best to create a completely separate document. As you have already learned via the roles and responsibilities section, we will need to indicate five distinct departments within the manuals we create. Those five departments are scheduling, human resources, quality assurance, marketing, and finance. I recommend developing a manual for each department, as well as a general operations manual.

The reason you need a general operations manual is because there are general operational aspects that everyone working at your company may need to understand. These matters may change over time, and as such, it is much easier to change one manual as opposed to five. For example, a common general operations manual may be time-tracking. Perhaps right now everyone submits their time worked via the old-fashioned, pen and paper, fill-in-the-blank timecard. Every employee does this regardless of their department, so it makes sense that teaching the employee "how-to" do their job would be a general operations manual item instead of just being in the Finance Department's manual, or copy-pasted into all five. Why isn't it in the handbook? Because the manual is a how-to guide, whereas the handbook contains your rules of employment.

Contrary to the advice I gave for the handbook about making the information as timeless as possible, the operation manuals need to be very detailed and will likely need to be edited frequently. While that is true, the frequency is nothing close to weekly, but it wouldn't be unheard of to realize you are editing an item on a monthly or quarterly basis. Editing would only happen as needed, so you may have a season of editing something every few weeks and then a six-month stint where nothing changes. That is okay. The manual is meant to be a how-to guide, and its instructions and coverage of the duties of each role need to remain current. In order to get a breakdown of the manuals' setup, go to *The 24/7 Solution* website to access the *Manual Creation Outline* and example.

Manuals are a key part of what led our businesses to scale from one to seven locations in eight years, and helped us go from generating $350,000/month in revenue to $20.4 million annually. Once we had a manual for every department, we were able to scale from three locations to seven in just three years. The reason these manuals are such an integral part of helping a business scale successfully, as well as in helping run any business more efficiently, is because they provide team members with a place they know they can get answers. As they are onboarded, they are trained directly from this document, and they can refer to it every minute, hour, and day as they learn and execute tasks in their role. If they have a question, they are not inclined to ask their supervisor or a team member first, interrupting another individual's productivity. Instead, they seek the answers to their questions in the manual first, allowing everyone to stay focused on accomplishing their goals.

I know what some people may be thinking: "Man, they ran a really cold, siloed environment. Clearly no one was welcome to ask questions." That couldn't be farther from the truth. Our team members trusted and believed in one another greatly, and shared many joys and heartaches with one another. However, they didn't spend their time asking one another how to fill out a timesheet if it was a holiday. Instead, they asked about how one another's holiday celebrations went after turning in an accurate timesheet. See the difference?

Manuals work wonders for protecting and getting the most value out of your – and your team members' – time, but they take time on the front end. The key to constructive manual creation is getting your team members' support as you develop them. If you create the manuals by yourself, spending hours developing them, and then hand them to your team to use, you're likely to be very disappointed. Even if you have a special "lunch and learn" – treating the team to lunch and teaching them about the manuals – I can almost guarantee you that the manuals will be collecting dust on the shelf very soon. If you do not already utilize manuals in your business, you have to get your team members' buy-in on the idea from the start. Not only is this a smart move to ensure their ongoing utilization, it is also a much better use of your time as the owner.

To get started, set up a team event. If you are a smaller office, you may request that your team come in on a Saturday in exchange for a weekday off so that you can have uninterrupted time dedicated to the manual creation process. If you are a larger team, you can have your department heads scheduled to be unavailable for a day so that you can work offline and without interruptions. During this event, your goal is to establish a general operations manual. In order to do that, you will need to cast the vision you have for the remaining departments.

As you get into the weeds of the general operations manual and try to teach your team what it looks like, do not be afraid of the details. When I initiated this idea with my team, I called it McDonaldizing. Little did I know at the time, a sociologist by the name of George Ritzer wrote an entire book on the concept of modeling efficiencies after McDonald's. The book is titled *The McDonaldization of Society*.

For me, "McDonaldizing" the business was inspired by a solo trip I took to Italy in 2012. At the time, I was a sucker for the book *Eat, Pray, Love* and I couldn't wait to eat my way through Italy on a nomadic journey. I scheduled three weeks of travel, starting in Venice and ending in Sicily. Upon arrival, I spent six long hours, jet-lagged, with many well-meaning expatriates in Venice trying to help me find my hostel – all to no avail. I was immediately homesick.

My second week was plenty rocky as well. I experienced theft in Rome, then nearly missed my connecting flight to Venice. Comfort, safety, and home were all I craved at that point. I passed a McDonald's on my way to my hostel in Sicily. While McDonald's was not normally a treat for me at home, the nostalgia of a Big Mac and fries was the healing I sought. To my dismay, the menu was full of unrecognizable items alongside the go-to American classics. I feared my craving for home would remain unmet. Warily, I ordered my Big Mac, fries, and coke. I took my first bite, closed my eyes, and was gloriously at home.

I later learned about Hamburger University. Hamburger University is a training facility at the McDonald's Corporation global headquarters in Chicago, Illinois. It is a place where promising restaurant managers, mid-managers, and owner/operators are instructed. It is where individuals learn about McDonald's standards. The standards at McDonald's are so detailed that, instead of simply being taught the ingredients that go into making a Big Mac, you are trained on the proper order in which to place each ingredient on the bun. For example, a Big Mac's bottom bun needs to have Big Mac sauce, then onions, then lettuce, and so on. Failure to follow the exact order is a failure to meet the standards of the franchise.

This attention to detail and to the particulars of processes is what led me to have the same experience at their establishment in Italy as I did growing up in Kentucky. This experience is what later inspired my desire to "McDonaldize" the manuals in my business, and ensure that if one administrative team member took a call about a given topic, they would handle it just the same as their peers two states away.

Utilizing the *Manual Creation Outline* available through *The 24/7 Solution* website, it is time to take your team through this exercise.

24/7 SOLUTION TIME

Acknowledgement Forms

There are a variety of acknowledgment forms you may need on record. One in particular is a wage acknowledgement form – something on file that your team member has signed to acknowledge their understanding of their pay. This is an opportunity for you to also promote the value of the employee's benefits, along with their salary. You can also use this document to emphasize any special caveats you have made for this team member without needing to edit the job description. For example, did you negotiate with them so they would only have to be on call one time a month, unlike their fellow team members? If so, this would be a good spot to acknowledge this stipulation. (Although, I don't recommend flexing too much with regard to on-call responsibilities. This can be hard to keep up with as a supervisor, and can cause issues of favoritism to develop among staff.)

Having a wage acknowledgement form that outlines benefits and potential earnings might be composed of parts including the information soon to follow. I have provided an example form for an employee compensated at $50,000/year with an opportunity for a monthly bonus* to be earned below.

Monthly Bonus Met Twice in One Year

$50,000	Base Salary
$4,800	On-Call Compensation
$1,000	Monthly Bonus
$2,000	401K Match
$12,000	Health Insurance Premium
$69,800	Total Potential Compensation

Monthly Bonus Met Six Times in One Year

$50,000	Base Salary
$4,800	On-Call Compensation
$3,000	Monthly Bonus
$2,000	401K Match
$12,000	Health Insurance Premium
$71,800	Total Potential Compensation

Monthly Bonus Met Twelve Times in One Year

$50,000	Base Salary
$4,800	On-Call Compensation
$6,000	Monthly Bonus
$2,000	401K Match
$12,000	Health Insurance Premium
$74,800	Total Potential Compensation

*EI & Company's suggested bonus structure is referenced in the Accountability Chapter

Having a wage acknowledgment form list out the compensation with the potential earnings/compensation identified is very helpful for your new team member and further helpful for you. Laying out for your team member how much you are potentially investing in them shows them how much you value them beyond their base pay. It is important to label this compensation as *potential* compensation. Failure to do so will tie you to providing them with compensation that may be much higher than you can afford (assuming certain criteria are not met). Furthermore, you'll want to make a note that the monthly bonus is outlined in a different document by saying something along the lines of "See 'Bonus Policy' for details."

Referencing your bonus policy on a different document provides you protection in two ways. One: it makes no guarantee that a bonus is a requirement from you as the employer. Two: it allows the bonus to be subject to changes. Putting the details of the bonus on the wage acknowledgment form will trap you into something you may not be able to honor later. However, casting out this vision for your new employee can be done safely as long as it is defined as "potential" earnings/compensation versus "guaranteed." My website has an editable version of a *Wage Acknowledgment Form* you can adapt for your business.

Another easy way to implement the "24/7 Solution" through the use of the *Wage Acknowledgement Form* is by including a thirty-day notice. We stated something along the lines of, "As an administrative team member you understand the value of your role in the lives of our clients and caregivers. As such, you understand a thirty-day notice is required in order to leave the company in good standing." You just gave yourself a couple of weeks longer to solve for turnover even if you hope this person never leaves.

As we previously discussed, other acknowledgment forms can save your employee from unnecessary hand cramps. Instead of having your employee sign a separate form each to agree to your business' absentee policy, dress code, and timekeeping expectations, you can provide them with a handbook that covers all of this important information and follow it up with a single acknowledgment form for the employee to sign to indicate their understanding of the rules of employment listed therein.

It is important to note that there are policies that may warrant a separate signature to draw your employees' attention. Some such policies include your confidentiality agreement and social media policy. Both can carry a great deal of weight in protecting your clients and your business, so placing extra emphasis on them by having a distinct document for your employee to sign separately will potentially demonstrate their importance to your employee. Many owners would say everything is important; I would agree. However, some policies place your business at greater risk if they are violated, and some are potentially more likely to be breached than others, so it may be important to draw attention to those matters. For example, though theft from a client is possible, it is not as probable as a caregiver taking a selfie with a favorite client and posting it on social media.

Let's imagine a worst-case scenario for your company: you learn that a kindhearted, albeit impulsive, caregiver posted a video of her and her client on social media. Within a short period of time, the video goes viral, and an estranged nephew sees his aunt. One thing leads to another, and now this estranged nephew is able to come back into his aunt's life and steals all of her life savings. Your business could be liable. If this could have been stopped by educating this kindhearted caregiver on the importance of confidentiality and social media through the handbook, and by providing her with a separate form to sign, then why wouldn't you make that effort? Let's continue the scenario: time has passed and the statute of limitations are just about to be met, and the family decides to sue you for employing this impulsive caregiver for exposing their loved one's identity. As your attorney works to defend your business, they will have a much easier time defending your case if there is a thorough handbook and a signed, specialized acknowledgment form.

In addition to having an acknowledgment form for your handbooks, it is important to have them for any manuals you may require your team members to utilize. The *24/7 Solution* website provides an example of a simple to understand, easy to adapt acknowledgment form. Acknowledgment forms are sometimes the only protection you have as an employer. Now, it is time to evaluate which acknowledgment forms your company is missing and create them.

24/7 SOLUTION TIME

Training Sign-Offs

Training sign-offs were inspired by the training skills checklist many Certified Nursing Assistant programs utilize before individuals receive their certification. Knowing that a CNA was required to complete a bed bath under the observation of an instructor, and that instructor was required to sign their name next to the skill, we implemented a similar process with our caregivers and then with our administrative staff. Training sign offs provide the business further protection, but, beyond that, they set your team members up for success.

In 2007, I began as a caregiver and was sent off to work with my first client after three and a half hours of orientation. That orientation included a video on how to assist with a few ADLs, but it mostly taught me how to be a good employee. Very little of that time was spent teaching me how to be a good *caregiver*. After I was promoted, I made it a goal to greatly revamp the orientation process for our caregivers.

After hosting a handful of focus groups with new and old caregivers, I gathered enough data that showed I wasn't the only one disappointed by the onboarding process. I began to make changes, but before I finalized everything, I conducted a blind survey of a majority of our caregivers and learned that most of them did not feel trained. After all of the data was collected, I made many changes, two of which were the implementation of training sign-offs at the completion of hands-on training over how to support ADLs. Secondly, we stopped calling the process "orientation" and began calling it "orientation and training." What was once three and a half hours was now carrying over into two days, totaling twelve to fourteen hours. When we invited our new caregivers to join us, they were invited to orientation on day one and training on day two. Six months later, we surveyed all of our newer caregivers using the same blind survey; 100% of them stated they felt they were well-trained.

Utilizing the training sign-off process with caregivers was a short jump from CNA training. Although training for an administrative role is much different than a caregiver's, it isn't too much of a jump to apply this process to the administrative role. The first bit of advice is to remember that common sense is not all that common. Do not assume that a certain skill is a no-brainer and doesn't warrant a sign-off. If your team member is going to potentially answer the office phone, they need to be trained and signed off on "how to answer the phone professionally" and trained on "how to manage the phone system." More is better.

It's important that you do not implement this process haphazardly. If you commit to having an employee make training sign-offs, you must follow all the way through with this process. It is also important that you do not just have a spot for your employee to initial or check off next to each item. Initialing and checking off is better than no training sign-off, but a signature is much better. You also need to have a date recorded next to each signature to denote the time when this employee showed completion of the task at hand. Next to their signature, you need to have a signature line for the trainer/supervisor to sign as well. Lastly, you'll need a signature line at the end of the form that acknowledges that all the training has been completed. Is this form overloaded with requests for signatures? Absolutely. Is it too much? Not at all, especially if you or your attorney are standing in front of a judge, defending your business.

Now it is time for you to develop your organization's training sign-offs.

24/7 SOLUTION TIME

Training Agenda

Every new staff member needs to be presented a training agenda on their first day with the company. If your organization has directors that report to you or your operations manager and they are hiring a direct report, the director needs to present the agenda to their supervisor for approval in advance of the new hire's first day. The training agenda needs to outline the new employees' first ninety days with the company, with a hyper-specific focus on the first thirty days and a more relaxed outline of the remaining sixty days. The first thirty days need to be developed to ensure every item on the training sign-off is accounted for, with blocked time to accomplish the training. For example, if your training sign-off is going to train on items A through Z; your agenda may look like this:

> Day 1 – A, B, C, F, G
> Day 2 – D, E, L, M, N
> Day 3 – O, P, Q, H
> Day 4 – etc.

For a more detailed training agenda example, go to www.the247solution.com and find the *Training Agenda Tool.*

Every Friday, a review of the week's training needs to occur. An easy way to accomplish this is by giving employees a pop quiz. This pop quiz is not intended to trip them up or make them feel uncomfortable. It is an opportunity to give them a safe space to test their knowledge, preparing them for their graduation from training, as well as giving their instructor insight on what training items need more time. This is why it's important to keep an open spot on the agenda for revisiting items. When developing the agenda, be conservative in what you believe you can accomplish. As you know, in the home care world, there are many factors that can influence the day's plans. It is always better to plan for fewer tasks to be trained versus packing too much into one day and getting behind. That is why developing the agenda before the new person's first day is so important. Having a roadmap for this new person that is prepared thoughtfully and ready to be presented to them from the get-go is key to their success.

With all of that said, be flexible. Recalibrate daily. Every day, you need to be on a path of progress. If some days derail completely because a no call, no show occurred, there is likely a later date on the agenda that speaks to training on how to handle this. If so, you'll move x in place of y and shift your agenda around. If you do not have an agenda to start, you'll always push off what is important and only ever handle what is urgent. This is especially true in the home care industry.

I have clients who have said, "Just get through the next twenty-four hours. We all know by tomorrow everything is going to change." Their team members, who have been in the industry longer than they have been owners, taught them this mentality. Due to the owner's inexperience, they allow this mentality to remain the predominant one. I call this mentality the "24 hour cog" mentality.

If you do not have an agenda to start, you'll always push off what is important and only ever handle what is urgent.

I came up with this play on words as I reflected on the effects this "next 24 hour mentality" had on my businesses and seeing the same effect on my clients' operations. A cog is a piece of machinery, well-oiled, that helps support the machine it is a part of in its overall function. The individuals working to get through the next twenty-four hours genuinely believed they were doing what was necessary to contribute to well-oiled operations, when, in reality, their approach was broken. Instead of oiling the cogs, they were replacing a broken one each day. They had been doing it this way for so long that they just assumed it was part of doing business in home care.

Instead of letting the business get bogged down, or as I liked to say *cogged* down, day in and day out by fixing broken cogs, clients can provide a bit of oil to keep things running smoothly. Once I can break through this mindset with a client and show them how to keep the cog well-oiled – freedom and capacity to grow occurs.

I liken that mindset to having dirty dishes. The dishes are dirtied every day due to the meals I have eaten. As I look upon them in the sink waiting to be cleaned, I could say, "What is the point? I'll just be eating food on them again tomorrow."

This mindset is silly, when you really think about it. Just because things may get messy or become disorganized the next day, the rational response to this challenge is to wash the dishes to get ahead of tomorrow's mess. The same is true for training agendas; recalibrating daily makes things that much less messy or disorganized the next day.

Are you a "leave the dirty dishes and eat off a dirty plate the next day" operation – the "24 hour cog" mentality? Or are you coming in every day to a clean kitchen and working on freshly-washed plates – the "24/7 Solution" mentality?

Operational Mentality	
 **24 HOUR COG**	 **24/7 SOLUTION TIME**
<ul><li>Reacting to interruptions.</li><li>Managing the next twenty-four hours or less.</li><li>Not having defined roles / excessive collaboration on solving problems.</li><li>Not creating or following a weekly/monthly/quarterly/ annual plan.</li><li>Spending time on busy work.</li><li>Allowing for venting versus problem solving.</li><li>Having meetings that could have been an email/call/text.</li><li>Reacting versus responding</li><li>Thinking short term versus long term.</li><li>Only thinking of goals on a macro level.</li></ul>	<ul><li>Responding versus reacting. Understanding the difference between crisis and an interruption then prioritizing accordingly.</li><li>Permitting "Do Not Disturb" project work.</li><li>Productive, time-managed meetings with action plans and deadlines.</li><li>Clearly defined roles and responsibilities with an appropriate amount of cross training.</li><li>Recognizing duplicatable systems and implementing ongoing processes.</li><li>Creating layers of back-up – having a deep bench.</li><li>Breaking down goals from macro to micro.</li><li>Developing a clear onboarding agenda for the first ninety days of employment with your organization.</li></ul>

Marcus Aurelius, a Roman emperor who ruled from 161 to 180 AD and who was a key figure within the Stoics, once said, "Don't be locked out of the rhythm any longer than necessary. You'll be able to keep the beat if you are constantly returning to it." In the case of training, "keeping the beat" entails returning to the original training agenda and training sign-off and making note of your progress. If you allow yourself to go off-course for very long, your new team member is going to fall into utter confusion. As the owner, you want to make sure your trainer is staying on track so that your new team member receives a warm welcome and a sense of security in their new role.

When the training agenda is originally developed, you need to work on it from the "24/7 Solution" mentality. Having this grounding document and honoring it fully is key to your team members' success. It not only limits the potential turnover from your administrative staff, but also sets a foundation that prepares employees to become future leaders. Modeling for them how to handle onboarding through this process is key for being able to scale your operations.

Throughout the entire training process, the new team member needs to be taking notes in the manual to better understand the step-by-step instructions for tasks which they are proving they can execute upon. When your manuals are written well, your team members are not forced to have every step memorized or written down in a notebook. Instead, they can utilize the table of contents to find the answer to their questions at any time. Streamlining this is key to an efficient business. Having these procedures in place makes all the difference in your ability as the owner or operator to work on your business versus work in your business.

With many of our clients, our biggest breakthrough is when we get them to stop playing whack-a-mole and finally get them to prevent moles from popping up in the first place. So, what are some common "moles?"

- Determining if a caregiver committed an offense meriting termination.
- Discovering that a client didn't receive care because a caregiver's schedule wasn't properly updated or edited.

- Making bad first impressions on a new client because team members didn't communicate properly about caregiver expectations.
- Having caregivers review out-of-date client profiles.

All of these are "moles" that can be whacked as they come up, but they can also be prevented from making their burrows in the first place – thanks to the "24/7 Solution" mentality. Proper onboarding helps prevent these problems, and it starts with recruiting, hiring, following a training agenda, and having a team member sign off that they will have ultimate ownership of the duties of their job.

On or close to day thirty, your new team member will need to meet with their trainer and the owner/operator to be fully signed off in their new role. It's important that this date is on the agenda and known by all parties from day one. This date is a target for both the trainer and the trainee. (I utilize the word "trainer" here because, in some cases, it may not be their direct supervisor.)

Now it is time to develop a training agenda template for future administrative team members. If you have a role you are in the process of hiring, prioritize an agenda for this role first and utilize that role's agenda as a template for future positions.

24/7 SOLUTION TIME

Certificate of Completion

The final step of the training process is often overlooked or made out to be a rather insignificant step. From an owner's or operator's chair, what matters most is that the new team member is trained and has signed off on their training. However, while getting your team member signed off does matter greatly to the business, a certificate of completion matters just as much or more to your new team member.

I once sat in a seminar where this question was repeatedly asked: "What if, every day, you walked into work you had first day jitters?" It doesn't take us long to forget our first day jitters; this is especially true as a worn-out home care owner and operator. I bet you have had opportunities to take a call from a potential client only for it to come at an incredibly inconvenient time and find yourself annoyed by the interruption. Remember when you first started your business? Remember how you sat there, hoping for that phone to ring so you could serve more seniors? If you cannot remember to have this mindset during your workday, that is okay, but I challenge you to remember that this newer team member is having their first experience with your company, and those first days and weeks are the most fundamental in determining the tone of their experience with your company.

Let's go back to the hunter-gatherer cycle analogy for a moment and remember our responsibility in bridging the disconnect from work to reward – but, this time, in the context of home care. While we can do this with our mission and core purpose, and of course later with their paycheck, we can find even more ways to do this throughout their employment experience. Do you remember your first week on a new job? Was your brain fried as you tried to obtain all the valuable information to do your job well and succeed for the business? The certificate of completion is a great way to reward them for their hard work during training and to show you appreciate them.

Home Care Hunter-Gatherer Cycle

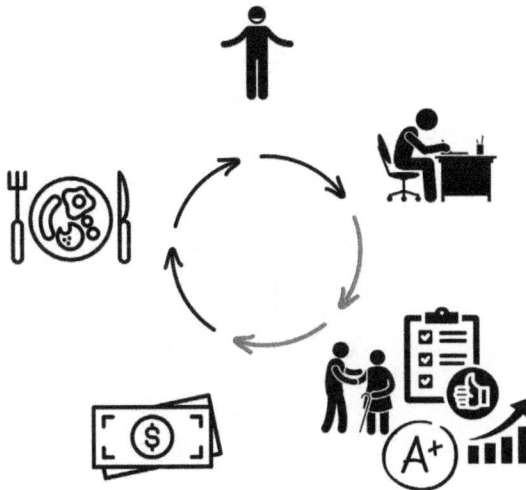

Beyond the recognition this provides your new team member, this ceremonial step serves as a milestone and recognition that they are now ready to face their job independently.

At this point in the process, your new team member should have gone through the following steps with your organization:

1. Recruited for a job they understood due to a clear job description.
2. Selected carefully.
3. Received rules of engagement through a handbook.
4. Trained with a very thorough manual they can reference and improve upon throughout their career.
5. Through the use of an agenda, they followed and signed a training sign-off to prove their competence and ability to be independent in their role.
6. Completed a final meeting with their trainer and the owner/operator to present their competence.
7. Received a certificate of completion to award them autonomy to function on behalf of the company in their role.

Each one of these "24/7 Solution" steps just helped you prevent 85% of the "moles" most owners tend to spend their time whacking, which means you get to put that time towards growing your business or making more time for your family.

Take a moment to create templates for your certificates of completion for each existing role you have on your team.

24/7 SOLUTION TIME

Now that you have completed your:

1. Job descriptions
2. Handbooks
3. Operation manuals
4. Acknowledgement forms
5. Training sign-offs
6. Training agenda
7. Certificate of completion

It is time to take your existing team through a roles and responsibilities reset. Although your team members likely participated in the creation of the above along the way, you still want evidence in their file that they are fully capable of the responsibilities of their role. The best way to do this is to develop a training agenda for each individual on your team and take them through the process of signing the training sign-off by showing you their ability to complete each skill. Once complete, each team member will then need to receive their certificate of completion. You could choose to do this for anyone hired moving forward, but I strongly recommend doing this with individuals currently on your team as well. This ensures they are clear on what is expected of them, shows them how to onboard any future direct reports they may have, and sets their file up to protect you as much as possible.

6

FINANCIALS

There are many aspects of a financially healthy business that are key to its success. Before you can evaluate your overhead and expenses thoroughly, though, you have to start by evaluating where you can price yourself in the market and where you land in terms of competitive pay. Before starting a business or making any major changes to your prices and wages, you need to start with a market analysis.

Market Analysis

You must keep your fingers on the pulse of your market relevance. Every week, your company is likely one of at least three companies that a family will be vetting. Even directly referred callers likely received direct referrals to more than one provider, or, before trusting their mom with just any care provider, they are backing up their referral with a quick internet search to screen other options.

It is likely that, when you first began your business, you took the time to research what your competitors were charging and how they structured their rates. This task is not a one and done task. I have worked with many owners, especially following the Covid-19 pandemic, who rushed to change their rates and wages before "mystery-shopping" the market. I get it. We were all gasping for air. Were we going to be considered essential, were we not? How deadly is this virus? Should we care for clients with Covid or not? And let's not revisit the horrors of contact tracing. Every day we were forced to react versus respond. That panicked reaction sometimes led to promises made to existing and future caregivers that could not be followed through on, as well as difficult rates for existing and potential clients. In some cases, home care owners began charging non-refundable start up fees upwards of $1,000. In other cases, we saw owners charging more on the weekends and passing the fee straight to the caregiver without covering their cost of services.

The situation of the home care market during the pandemic provides a dramatic example of emotions and survival driving the industry. Let's be careful not to sum up these poorly strategized decisions as a once-in-a-lifetime pandemic problem. Letting emotions and survival drive business decisions happened well before the pandemic, and will continue to happen. As referenced in the chapter on self-leadership, constantly reviewing your emotional intelligence, keeping it in balance, and continuing to educate yourself and raise your awareness can make all the difference in achieving profits now *and* profits later as opposed to a momentary blip in profit gains.

Regardless of the environment, most of the time, you have more time than you think. To return to the prehistoric analogy, we still believe we are being chased by a tiger or soon to be bitten by a snake, when in reality not many things in our first world environment are as life-threatening. I regularly aggravated my team members when they would rush into my office panicking about a situation that had come to their attention, barely able to get their words together. I would let them get to a pause, then step in and say, "Okay, look behind you."

If this was their first time hearing me say it, they'd either look at me, confused, or whirl around in a panic. Once they discovered nothing was behind them, they would ask me what they were supposed to find. I'd smile and say, "Do you see a tiger?"

Of course, the answer was always "no." Based on our relationship, they would appreciate the grounding, and then we'd do some problem solving to address their situation. What I did with my team members in these situations was the same thing I did for myself, constantly. It is no doubt the approach you need to take when struggling to hire caregivers and acquire new clients. Instead of thinking about your wages and rates the way you would a tiger, maybe it is time to recognize there *isn't* a tiger in the first place. Maybe, instead, you're simply being *cogged* down by a "24 hour cog" mentality and need to implement some "24/7 Solutions."

Now to the nuts and bolts of rate structures. Schedule yourself a semi-annual review of wages and rates, measuring yours against your top competitors'. As you either conduct or outsource these mystery shop calls, be sure to ask just enough questions to understand a little beyond the surface. There are many companies you can hire that will conduct these secret shopper calls for your business; we are one of them. If you are interested in this service, please visit *The 24/7 Solution* website to purchase a secret shopping survey of your competitors. The key things to achieve in the shop process are an understanding of rates, structure, and fees. Below, I'm going to elaborate on how to shop competitors based on these factors. As I provide you with questions to use to obtain this information about your competitor, begin to answer the same questions about your organization.

With this "24/7 Solution Time" stop, be sure to schedule your future market analysis calls and then conduct a market analysis of your top competitors. Keep in mind, your top competitors in employment may be different than your top competitors in service.

24/7 SOLUTION TIME

Rates

Rates for service are exactly what they sound like. How much per hour/per service does a business charge? The best way to acquire this information is to provide a hypothetical situation of a loved one who is presently of low acuity – meaning that they need minimal help each week – but based on their diagnosis, they will need higher acuity care soon. This will ensure you get a clear understanding of rates across the spectrum. It is not unusual for home care providers to be tight-lipped on the phone. In this case, you may only be able to get an overview of a range of costs that hits the low, high, and possibly average rates.

In certain states, you may learn that your competitors provide a wider scope of service than you do. This is another benefit of using the low acuity to high acuity scenario. As such, you may consider expanding or even minimizing your scope of services. Certain states may require much more from you if you expand. Similarly, you may have much less to do if you choose to simplify your services. Do not make this decision lightly; revisit the drawing board regularly before making the leap to expand or simplify your business.

Structure

Structure pertains to how you apply the rates. If the business is charging hourly, do they charge more for fewer hours a week than they charge larger hour clients? If the business uses a fee-for-service payment model, is there a minimum number of services per week they must receive? Do they ever transition from service to hours? Will they work with someone who is in hospice? If so, is there a higher charge? What if there are two individuals in the home needing care? Is there a higher charge? If so, under what circumstances? Are they providing live-in services? If so, how quickly can you convert to this service?

Fees

When it comes to your rate, structure, and fees, your goal is to remove as many barriers of entry to your services for the end user as possible. In addition, you need to do this while still protecting your business' financial health. In some cases, certain fees are necessary and unavoidable.

In one of our franchise territories, we had areas of service where we sometimes had to drive one and a half hours just to arrive at a potential client's home for a consultation. We called these areas *no man's land* because they were technically not a part of our territory – or any other neighboring franchise's territory. They were so rural not many providers were willing to service them due to challenges with staffing. In our effort to always help seniors, we would make the trek to service the seniors in *no man's land*. There were many times where these consultations were set up and confirmed, and I or another team member would make that drive, only to arrive and learn that they had *meant* to cancel for one reason or another. This meant that my team member or I had lost three plus hours of our week's availability to serve our existing clients and caregivers. This may be a very fair and reasonable place to charge a fee or deposit in advance for an otherwise free consultation. To be clear, we never did. Instead, we created a system with these more distant consultations to confirm our appointments in advance. If this had not solved our challenge, receiving a deposit would have been our next step.

Another example of a fee that may be applied for *no man's land* clients is one to compensate caregivers for the time spent driving to these remote locations. A successful way we handled this for our clients was through charging an extra hour or two for each shift. We had a baseline model of doing it this way. However, we would negotiate what was best for the business, the future caregiver, and the client whenever we had remote clients that needed our service. When these scenarios came up, my team was trained to explain that an hour at the start of the shift and an hour at the end of the shift would be charged as more than the other hours of care.

In addition to telling clients they were trained to evaluate the situation, my team would "call the manager" in some of these cases. After explaining the extra fees to the family, my team member and I would have a private conversation and see if there was room to negotiate. For example, if there was a 24/7 client needing care, the idea of charging four extra hours a day to cover two twelve hour shifts seemed unfair and unnecessary. However, a six hour shift four days a week likely warranted the two extra hours' pay to protect our caregiver.

Starting with the most expensive rate with the family and then "calling the manager," my team member would return to the meeting and let them know how much of an exception we could make to help them. This always led to our clients feeling valued and our services being personalized to their needs.

"Call the manager" came from the practice of a car salesperson. It's not uncommon knowledge that if you want to buy a car from a car salesperson and you ask for an exception or change to the deal, your salesperson will quickly respond, "Let me ask my manager." Whether they actually asked their manager or not, they would come back and meet you in the middle of your requested price. This technique exists because it works. Unlike the cliché sleazy car salesperson that many home care operators are afraid to be perceived as, we legitimately tried to do what was right for our client. Doing what is right, coupled with establishing unique financial business decisions in the hands of the operational leader, allowed our team to feel appreciated and confident in what we did for families.

It's important that, as you structure your rates, you find ways to make the client tell you "no" rather than you telling them "no." We'll dive into what that means more specifically in the "Phone Intake" section, but for the purposes of rate structure, it is not conducive to business growth to put up barrier after barrier for clients. The rates, structure, and fees should all be simple and easy to understand. Your client, or your client's decision-maker, should be able to pick up the phone, call their sibling, and rattle off rather quickly how much they need to budget for care and how it works. If your client's rate structure cannot be simplified and written on a Post-It note, you're losing clients and, in effect, losing revenue.

Wage Structure

Setting up your wage structure is very similar to managing your rate structure. If you are charging clients by the hour and paying your care-givers by the hour, it is very simple. As of 2024, the industry agrees on a two to one fee to pay for caregiving services. Before considering payroll taxes, worker's compensation insurance, or any other business expenses, you are working from a 50% gross margin. This means that if you charge your client $20.00 an hour, it is common to pay your average caregiver half of that rate – that is, $10.00. This never works out exactly every time. If you have had a caregiver on staff for two or more years, you have likely offered them pay increases over time, and your rate increases may not have kept up with those pay increases. That is okay; it is not worth micromanaging every caregiver to every client. Instead, you want to always shoot for an average gross margin of 50% minimum.

Evaluating your competitor's client rates is only half the battle. You cannot make a sound business decision on client rates without also evaluating your top competitor's caregiver wages and structure. It's important to ask your HR team who they believe are the top home care competitors in your organization's territory. It is not uncommon for the names of competitors given by HR to be different from the names given by Marketing. The best way to evaluate your competitors' wages is to conduct a mystery shop call as a potential employee. There are many companies that can do this for you, including mine, but this need is sometimes addressed best by your recruiter. Having your recruiter get a perspective on how competitors handle these calls, whether good or bad, can help them learn what to do better or what they should keep doing when it comes to potential employees. Provide your recruiter with the *Wage Evaluation Tool* that can be found on my website to help evaluate your competitor's wages and benefits.

There are a variety of ways to structure pay. Here are some common approaches and things to keep in mind as you consider which one to take:

Pay	Considerations
Weekend and Third Shift Differential	▪ Need to charge clients more for weekends and third shifts to compensate, or charge more than the 2:1 ratio for weekday hours to balance out the difference. ▪ Once you make this business decision, it is very difficult to undo. ▪ Do not make this rate/pay decision from a "24 hour cog" mentality.
Pay Lower Rate to Allow for "Sleepover" Shifts versus "Stay Awake" Shifts.	▪ Clients need to agree to this and understand they receive a lower fee because they accept the mutual risk of the caregiver being asleep. ▪ Clients may choose the lower rate at risk of their safety, and your team may not be equipped to convince them otherwise.
Live-In	▪ Clients need to understand the cost savings lead to less flexibility in caregivers. If they are unsatisfied with a caregiver, it may take four to six weeks to find a more suitable replacement. ▪ Overtime must be evaluated in the cost. ▪ Recruiting and finding available caregivers can be very challenging, minimizing the pool of qualified matches.
Higher Wage for Greater Experience/ Higher-Skilled	▪ Will you charge the client for higher acuity care? If so, will you only match more experienced caregivers to these clients? ▪ How are you evaluating the potential caregivers' experience?

There are many points to consider when evaluating pay and setting up wage structures to cover the demands of the business. The above items are just a few. Be sure to check with your franchisor or an attorney about specific laws in your state and to make sure you are compensating employees properly.

Today things have become much more complex than they were prior to the changes with Companionship Exemption. Overtime and drive time have become more complicated to manage, and many offices have battled the Department of Labor and lost. Do not assume you are doing things right; seek clarification and always inspect your software. The job of the software supplier is to provide software to help you run your business. They are not responsible for knowing the latest updates to employment laws. Even if they promise that they are experts in paying your employees in this industry, always verify this by digging and asking questions. You are the owner of your business and, whether they promise optimal outcomes or not, it is your neck on the line if the software fails to deliver.

Now that you have completed a thorough market analysis of wages and rate you are ready to make decisions for your business, utilize this *Wage/Rate Roadmap* tool from www.the247solution.com to establish changes you will make in your business and your execution timeline.

24/7 SOLUTION TIME

7

CLIENT ACQUISITION

There are four pillars you need to have in place to have a successful home care business. All four need to be standing on stable ground.

Unfortunately, many owners are running around these four pillars, rushing to push a falling pillar back towards stability. Grunting with all their might to stabilize one pillar, they tend to overcompensate and cause further instability.

I see this so often with my clients. They haven't lost sight of their why, but because of their failure to have roles, responsibilities, policies, and procedures in place, the pillars are standing on unstable ground. This unstable ground causes pillars to begin to fall. Establishing a clear organizational structure to stabilize these four pillars is a must so that all four are addressed and valued equally. If you are not sure where to start, go back to the "Roles and Responsibilities" chapter for support. The first pillar we are going to dive into a deeper explanation of is *client acquisition*. Before we get started, though, keep in mind that no single pillar is of greater importance than another.

Intake

A common mistake owners make is referring away business. They've established their business' boundaries, such as establishing that they are a more acute care provider and requiring certain minimal hours. While I agree with the latter tactic, I'll never agree with the former and referring away business. My team was trained to recognize that, if someone calls to ask where they can get a hospital bed, then they probably also need home care. Instead of answering their question and moving on, my team was trained to learn more about their case and tell them how our services can help with their situation. The same was true for someone who might call and say they only need transportation once or twice a week. The assumption that was embedded into my team was that we could help them, regardless of our boundaries on service.

Something we learned at one of our more pivotal points as a business was how to get the customer to tell us "no," as opposed to us saying "no" to them. I reference this concept in the "Financials" chapter, under the *Fees* section, but now we are going to dive deeper into it. When we learned this lesson, we were serving around 20,000 to 25,000 hours a month between our two offices and we couldn't seem to grow more than 1-3% over the course of a few months. As a business that was used to double digit growth annually, this felt like a plateau. We had not placed weekly minimum expectations on our services and, every Friday, we were working well past 8 p.m. to get the weekend covered. In our effort to always put the customer first, we sacrificed everyone else's feelings and wellbeing, including our own. We had to take a long, hard look at what that mentality was doing to us and our team members.

Putting emotions aside and looking at the open shifts on the calendar, we found our pain point. The shifts keeping us working late at night were for clients who only needed us a few hours a week, and most often needed us at, what one may call, a clunky time of day, such as 10:00 a.m. to 2:00 p.m., or 3:00 p.m. to 7:00 p.m.

After many difficult, late Friday nights and a continued observation of this pattern, we made a decision to take care of our clients *and* team members equally. From that point forward, we knew we needed to have a minimum hours per week commitment for clients. As we went to the drawing board and conducted a market analysis, we decided on a twelve-hour per week minimum. This isn't unheard of, and is something you see almost everywhere now. However, the common mistake I referenced at the beginning of this section is where we made a different choice. Our choice was the difference between a "24 hour cog" mentality and a "24/7 Solution" mentality.

Instead of referring clients who did not meet our weekly minimum request to other businesses and losing potential revenue, we would process these prospects just the same. We would invest in them with the same attention as we would a potential 24/7 client, which meant we scheduled an in-home consultation to learn more about their needs. A quick point of clarity: we always made sure any in-home consultation was conducted *after* the prospect was provided our rate ranges over the phone. We wanted to make sure the caller knew the range of rates possible for their care and that most of our care was paid for privately before setting up an in-home consultation. However, we never homed in on their final rate. We would simply say our rate range and let them know the in-home consultation would help us determine where they fall within our rates. If they pressed us, we might answer with something like, "You're likely to fall at X/hour, but it is hard to say without a thorough review of your care needs." By saying it this way, we always left the door open for an in-home consultation to determine an individual's final rates.

Once we were in the home, our job was to be the expert in home care. As I told every new team member in training, "you know this company better than anyone on the other end of the call." It is so common for team members to be intimidated by the caller on the other end of the line. This intimidation may be because the caller is a doctor, lawyer, hospital administrator, or someone who seems very put together. Regardless, that person is calling for your help, to learn about something you or one of your team members know more about. It is important to always present yourself as an expert for your company and in home care. Even as the expert for your company, you may run into questions for which you will need to find answers. It is okay to admit to the caller that you need to find out a particular detail and communicate a plan to follow up with an answer.

As experts in home care, we utilized our time to consult on the need for home care. We would take them through a care evaluation that ranged from fill in the blank fields, like date of birth and emergency contacts, to open-ended deep dives into their medical history or a day in the life for them. By the time the paperwork was complete, it allowed our team member to walk through a thorough care evaluation and provide a *professional recommendation* for care. About 60% of the time, someone calling for *as needed* care would inevitably need a regular schedule of care. About 90% of the time, someone calling for care a couple of times a week now had evidence pointing them towards the importance of having more days of care a week.

In the event a client still did not make sense for a schedule within our weekly minimums, we would explain their care fell at a higher rate. This idea was born during late night talks with my neighbor. As a general contractor, he traveled throughout the United States building restaurants for a lot of successful franchises – Cracker Barrel, CookOut, McDonald's, and Rafferty's were a few of his main contracts. While he was capable of building houses and doing other construction work, he made more income from restaurants and had more consistent hours working on them. Whenever a request to build a house came across his desk, he never said "no;" instead, he would double and sometimes triple his labor costs when providing the estimate for him to do the work. If he could stay in town and build this house for the same rate he would get if he built a restaurant out of town, he would gladly stay in town to do it. Essentially, he charged more to do the work he didn't want to do. If they decided to pay it, it was a win-win.

This is not to say that you do not want to provide care to a senior needing five hours a week, but, as a business owner, it's important to remember how your team members and especially caregivers are spending their time. If the client is willing to pay double, the charge for not meeting your weekly minimums, then it's a win-win: a client receiving care and a margin you can afford. Furthermore, you have a client in your pipeline receiving care and building trust with your company – *not* a competitor. This is why it is so important to make prospects say "no" to you, versus saying "no" to them. Every five-hour-a-week client is a client whose care needs will increase, and not telling them "no" ensures you will be there as an option for them when the need for 24/7 care arises.

I have clients today that have found more "24/7 Solutions" to making a prospect say "no" to care as opposed to having to say "no" to them. There are a lot of ways to solve this problem, but the overall point still remains: find a way to protect your business while still providing a service that meets the needs of your clients.

Go to *The 24/7 Solution* website to get a copy of our *Care Evaluation,* which helps prescribe care to seniors in need. Utilize this document to learn and then teach your team how to become expert care evaluators.

24/7 SOLUTION TIME

Starting Care

Now that we have established care with a client, we need to follow through on meeting our commitments and continuing to be positioned as the expert in home care. So often, the time between a consultation with the family and the first shift is where things go incredibly wrong. There are so many opportunities for errors or for balls to be dropped, and it's important that you establish a clear system to prevent these mistakes from happening. The use of a checklist at this stage is key. You can go to my website and download the *New Client Checklist.* At the very least, you want your checklist to include the following:

- Contact Scheduling Department to inform of new case high-lights and start date.
- Update software with profile information:
  o DOB
  o Emergency Contacts
  o Billing Information
  o Schedule

Oftentimes, the ball is dropped at the scheduling phase: either the scheduler matches a caregiver who is already (or should be) on their final warning with the company due to poor work performance, or on the client's first day of care where they need help to a doctor's appointment, they send a non-driving caregiver. It's important that there is an accountability system in place for the individual who conducted the consultation that helps guard against these types of errors. Here is a sample of a *New Client Email* a team member would often send after signing a new client. It was part of the checklist we utilized for new client starts:

Subject Line: New Client – Joe Smith

Body of Email:

> (Greeting) Hi everyone!
>
> I'm excited to welcome another client to our care and help one more person have a better experience at home!
>
> (Key Notes:) We signed up Mr. Joe Smith for care beginning this Friday at 1 p.m. Mr. Smith has previously been working with a competitor who had a history of not showing up or calling to say they could not send a replacement. I have promised them we would not drop the ball in communication on this matter so I have made it a requirement that we have a staff member there to introduce any future new caregivers. I've also explained to them that we will be there on Friday for their first shift to make sure it gets started on the right foot.

Main needs: meal prep, med reminders, shower assistance.

Physical Limitations: memory challenges, otherwise ambulatory.

(Ask:) Scheduling please reply all with the name of the caregiver who will be serving Mr. Smith this Friday.

(Closing) Name

This system would ensure that a client was given special notice. There is no way that the team could say they didn't know they had a new client, no way they could say they didn't know his basic needs or when he was needing care, and no way they could say they were not asked to set a good example. The first thought in your mind upon reading this may be, *We don't have time to do that along with everything else we already have on our plate!* I get it, but I would argue, you don't have time not to do it. While it is one more thing to do, this step ensures full clarity for your entire team, holds the scheduling team accountable to the entire team, and provides an opportunity for individuals to remember why they started working in home care in the first place! Contrary to first impressions, this *extra* step is actually a "24/7 Solution," not a "24 hour cog."

Once this step has been taken, you will still need to make sure you keep up with the shift being scheduled with a quality match. As a part of the checklist for the new client start, you may have a spot where you will require the individual who conducted the consultation to mark their calendar and follow up with scheduling by a certain time and date. Teaching these expectations and making them second nature is what leads home care businesses to become the best in the industry. This is not micromanagement; this is setting clear expectations about standards and then following up to ensure these standards are being met. When this individual checks with scheduling and learns the assignment hasn't been filled, they will then know to check in later or be a team player and find a way to further support this client in having an exceptional initial experience with your office.

As mentioned in the sample *New Client Email*, you may require a staff member to be onsite with the new caregiver. In my entire time overseeing home care operations, this was never missed. While speaking at conferences, I have heard a handful of people scoff when this is stated. I can only imagine it is because it is too hard to believe. However, I guarantee you it was true. If a client was starting care with our services, there was no other way for care to begin than to have an administrative member onsite to introduce the caregiver. This introduction is key. By conducting an introduction, you ensure the following:

1. Someone from your team is onsite at the start of the shift to ensure the reliability of the company is demonstrated.
2. A client receives a warm introduction to ease their nerves.
3. A caregiver is prepped in person and in private on how to create an exceptional experience for the client. This private conversation alone elevates the expectations of quality service.
4. A caregiver receives a warm introduction to ease their nerves.
5. The administrative team member completes a tour of the home with the caregiver to make sure all questions can be answered to meet the goals of the shift.
6. Again, someone from your team is onsite at the start of the shift. This provides insurance in coverage. If a caregiver fails to arrive, the administrative team member can immediately begin providing care.

Before continuing, you need to determine how you can improve your client's experience. How can new clients with your company go from satisfied to delighted and become advocates of your services? Take a moment to develop your *New Client Checklist*, which will help ensure that the logistics of your clients' care are managed well and set up for success.

24/7 SOLUTION TIME

First Week of Care

Now that your client has gone through their first shift with your company, it's important to make sure they were happy with the day's events. When you teach your team to check on the quality of service, it's important that you don't lead them down the path of only being customer service-minded. While it is important to have a customer service hat on and make sure the client is satisfied, it's equally important to remember that you and your team are experts in home care and on the services you provide. The saying "the customer is always right" is not always true for senior care clients. Through consistent training, your team can discern between when the customer (client) is right and when you are adequately providing the services the client needs. For the team members you entrust with checking on quality, their ability to hold these two things in balance is very important.

With that said, it's vital to have a system in place to follow up with your client following their initial shift with your company. Go to www.the247solution.com for a *New Client Follow Up Form* to use as a guide on the best questions to ask. Keep in mind that this form will be of no use if the follow-up is not conducted within the first twenty-four business hours following the initial shift.

It's important that your team checks in early and frequently at the beginning of care. This helps your organization get ahead of any concerns that may start to boil up. Even at our best, it is nearly impossible to have a full picture of what care in the home will need to look like from an initial, and even thorough, consultation. These calls are opportunities to check on satisfaction, but also, more importantly, to recalibrate care in a way that helps a senior have quality support. Recalibrating care is only possible when you stand confidently as an expert in home care. In the *New Client Follow Up Form*, we also give equal value to the office's relationship with the client's family. We hold in balance the following things:

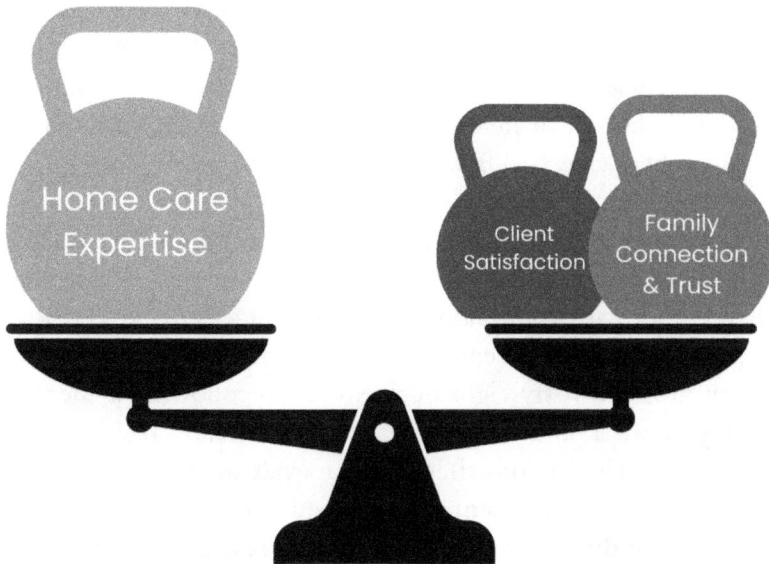

The way to build trust and connection with the family is to reach out. At the time of the initial consultation, it's important to always get all the client's children's names and contact information. During my time overseeing operations, we sadly encountered one too many times where a child was outlived by their parent. This meant the connection we built with the primary family caregiver was lost. It wasn't uncommon in this situation for another child to swoop in out of necessity and grief and move their parent into a facility, or into their home hundreds of miles away. Because of the circumstances, the client's quality of life was not able to be fully considered.

After this happened enough times, we changed our process and decided we would always get the names and contact information of every child at the beginning of care. After services began, we would make a concerted effort to call and introduce ourselves to each one. The conversation or message would be as simple as something like this:

Hi Susie, My name is _____. I am the _____ with _____ home care. I am reaching out because we began care with your mother today and, after talking with her, your sister, and our caregiver, things appear to be off to a great start. We are excited to be able to provide your mother with services that will keep her independent and safe in her home. I just wanted to introduce myself and let you know I am here in case you ever have any questions about your mother's care. Feel free to call/text me at _____-_____-_____.

Following a voicemail, it's important to send a short text about why you were calling and then follow up with an email. Providing this family member with your team member's contact info in as many formats as possible is key. Keep in mind, all of this needs to occur within the twenty-four to forty-eight business hours following a client's first shift. If you are a smaller organization and already feel like you are running on a skeleton crew then you can evaluate which clients would receive this premier treatment at the consultation. Once decided, identify these individuals in your software by creating a tagging system such as "VIP."

You have the luxury to define and teach your team what constitutes a VIP tag. It may reflect the revenue impact their care has on your business. In other words, are they eighty-four to one hundred and sixty-eight hours a week in care? Similarly, it may be their *potential* revenue impact. Are they a long-term care insurance client with a generous policy who is just now beginning their senior care journey?

You may also consider someone a VIP client because of their potential to be problematic. In many facets of business where ongoing clients are involved, there can be problem clients and there can be dream clients. The best way to manage a problem client is to identify them and always hit their problems head on. It is very easy to want to avoid these clients, but avoiding them only makes the problems worse. You may have heard the aphorism, "What we resist, persists." This is very true when it comes to problematic clients.

It's important to remind your team that no one client is more valuable than the other as a human being. That is not what is meant by VIP. However, it is important to remind the team that some clients' revenues and time expenditures cost the company more money if not managed well.

After the first shift follow up, you have another few steps to take before placing a client into your ongoing quality assurance rotation. After one week of service, the next step is to follow up in nearly the same fashion as you conducted the initial follow up. The only difference this time is that you do not need to contact every child; you've made your support known at this point, and now, it is time to work with the primary decision-maker. The *New Client Follow Up Form* will speak to this, but, in short, you will want to contact the caregiver who has been with that client most, the client – if they are cognitively able to speak for themselves – and the primary family member contact/decision-maker. After this process is complete, you can now file the *New Client Follow Up Form*.

I realize that killing trees and using paper is potentially old-fashioned and not conducive to remote work. However, there are a few procedures that are too important to place in a digital file. I've heard all the arguments for doing client follow-ups digitally, but the reality is that rarely will a digital file be remembered and followed. You will forget or ignore its existence. A form sitting on your desk forces your brain to notice it. This brings up another issue: if your desk is a pile of books and papers and you can barely find a clean place to sit your coffee cup in the morning, you have bigger problems to solve. Once those problems are solved, then you can implement the *New Client Form* process. There is nothing more important to a home care business' success with a client than the way the first thirty days of care are handled.

Now that we have evaluated the best way to delight your clients, it is your turn to determine which steps you will implement in your business. Utilize the *New Client Follow Up Form* and customize it to your clients' needs and your organization's capabilities.

24/7 SOLUTION TIME

8

CLIENT RETENTION

The only time the order of the pillars mentioned in the previous chapter matters is during the small period of time when you are waiting to start your first client. Otherwise, all four pillars carry the same value and deserve equal attention. Once a client trusts your services, it is time to ensure they stay. You often hear about customer satisfaction, ensuring your clients are satisfied. We always trained our staff to not only satisfy our clients but to leave them

> **Satisfied customers don't complain, while advocates cannot wait to tell everyone how thankful they are for your services.**

delighted. In Ken Blanchard's and Sheldon Bowles' book, *Raving Fans*, they demonstrate how satisfied customers just aren't good enough. Our goal was to create advocates, not just satisfied customers. Satisfied customers don't complain, while advocates cannot wait to tell everyone how thankful they are for your services. There is a major difference between the two and, sometimes, it only takes you making a few minimal additions to your services to start producing advocate clients.

Preventative Care

Now that care has begun successfully, it is time to continue your client's journey of aging in place. In 2007, the idea of home care was still a foreign concept. As I've mentioned before, when I became a care-giver, I was shocked that I was getting paid to provide such a service. As a new professional industry, we were still trying to figure out how to meet our clients' needs. If a prospective client called and needed transportation to a doctor's appointment, we were the solution. If a prospective client called and needed light housekeeping two to three times a week to take care of laundry and other miscellaneous needs, like their cat's litter box, we were the solution. If a prospective client wanted assistance with their breakfast and lunch, we were the solution. Essentially, callers, seniors, and family members alike were telling us how we could serve their needs. As we marketed our services in the early days, we actually had a list of sixty services we offered that ranged from vacuuming to checking the mail.

Over the years, the needs of our clients have changed. The home care industry has become much more than just a "sitter" service. While we would serve those sixty needs and more, we came to realize we were so much more than a bulleted list of services. I still remember Paul Hogan, founder of Home Instead, standing on stage and shar-ing a story about the day one of his caregivers enlightened him about home care being much more than companionship and help at home. Home Instead began on June 1, 1994 in his grandmother's home. By June of 1995, they had sold their first franchise and, fast forward to my last day with Home Instead, there were nearly 700 franchises nationally and almost 400 more internationally. All along the way, Paul had his ear to the ground.

I remember Paul standing on stage and admitting to the audience of over 1,000 franchise conference attendees that a caregiver taught him that Home Instead was so much more than a list of sixty services being provided in a senior's home. He told a story about a senior who advanced in care so much that the family had no other choice than to move her into a skilled facility to manage her advanced medical needs. As he stood on the porch with the caregiver and discussed this next step for the client's life, he looked at her and said, "Thank you for all you have done for this client. The office will be in touch with you on finding you a new client, she was so lucky to have you help her for all this time."

It was then that the caregiver looked at him and said, "Our services are not done. I am going to be by her side every day in that facility, making sure she gets every need met. I am going to make sure she never feels alone inside of those four walls. I will be holding her hand until her last breath."

As time continued, it became more and more evident to home care providers that we were much more than sitters. As our clients' needs evolved, so did our ability to stand as experts in the industry. What was once previously a brochure listing over sixty services for people to look through to address possible needs became a consultative service, where we recommended our services based on our evaluations of what the client needed to age in place. Beyond the intake process, you have to continue this evaluation as you provide care to a senior. As a part of your quality assurance approach, find a way to make aging in place top of mind.

What always really helped drive this point home with my team was to compare what we do to a dentist's work. When we go to the dentist with pain in a tooth, we do not tell the dentist how to fix it. We arrive and tell them the pain we are experiencing, then the dentist diagnoses the problem and prescribes the solution. Whether we accept their prescription and apply it is up to us. It is not the dentist's job to decide what we will do; it is their job to tell us how to fix our pain. This is the gap home care professionals fail to bridge. It is not our job to decide what a client needs to do. It is our job to tell our clients how they can address their pain points.

For whatever reason, we feel bad recommending that a senior use more of our services. There is a disconnect between the need and the prescription, and I cannot quite name the reason why that is. I think we often fall into the trap of feeling bad for charging the client more money; we know that our services come with a price. However, the dentist doesn't hesitate in telling you about a cavity that needs to be filled just because it may cost you money. A car mechanic doesn't fail to tell you that you need to replace a belt just because it will cost you money. A plumber doesn't decide not to share that the pipes need to be replaced just because his labor and the equipment will cost you money. So why do we?

As home care experts, it is our job to learn what our client's pain points are. While they may be telling us our care is only needed three days a week for meals because their mom is losing weight, we may learn through our diagnosis process that she is also failing to take her medication every morning. As such, we need to prescribe a solution that addresses the overall diagnosis of the client's pain. This concept is true not only during intake, but also throughout your client's time with the organization. Every time your team member goes into the home to assess the client's satisfaction and needs, they need to be considering what they need to prescribe, or as we put it, professionally recommend.

To age in place, a senior needs your expertise, and needs you to be looking around the corner on their behalf. Regardless of how long you have been a business owner, or how long your team member has been an employee, your organization knows more about your business' services than the client. You are the expert. As you evaluate a client's needs, you may come across a situation like this:

> *A client has had seven-day-a-week care from 8:00 a.m. – 3:00 p.m. for two years. They needed help with getting their day started, breakfast, and lunch, and didn't need any support at night, because they have always eaten peanut butter crackers for dinner and been able to get themselves to bed. As you evaluate the services you are providing, you ask the primary caregiver educated questions and evaluate the client's overall health. You come to learn that the nighttime routine is becoming more challenging. The caregiver walked in and found that the client had left the doors unlocked to the home, forgot to shut the garage door, and was asleep in her recliner on multiple occasions. Furthermore, the client has become more and more incontinent and the Depends she is wearing are always soaked.*

After uncovering this information, it is your job as the expert to prescribe your professional recommendation. How do we do our part as professionals to let the client or decision-maker know they have a "cavity" before it's too late?

My recommendation is to follow the steps below when speaking on the phone with the decision-maker.

1. Greeting
2. Pleasantries

3. Reason for calling
4. Acknowledge care history
5. Findings
6. Provide professional recommendation
7. Result
8. Effective date
9. Close
10. Follow-up plan

Utilizing the scenario above, such a conversation may look something like this:

- Greeting - *Hi Kathy!*
- Pleasantries - *I wanted to let you know I went to see your mom today. It was so good to see how she and Susie get along, and I was lucky enough to hear her sing while Susie played the piano!*
- Reason for calling. - *I wanted to let you know what I learned from my evaluation.*
- Acknowledge Care History - *As you know, your mom has needed care from 8:00 a.m. to 3:00 p.m. for the past two years and that has met her needs.*
- Findings - *As I spoke with Susie privately, I learned of a few concerns that I wanted to bring to your attention.*
- List concerns.
- Provide Professional Recommendation – *It is my professional recommendation that you increase your mom's care to include 6:00 p.m. to 10:00 p.m. every night.*
- Result – *The goal of this increase would be to ensure that your mom…*
- Explain benefits of this change.
- Effective Date – *One of our evening caregivers, Julie, who has been with your mom before, would be ready to begin on Tuesday.*
- Close – *Do you have any concerns regarding this change in schedule?*
- Follow Up Plan – *I'm going to reach out to you on Friday to let you know how the adjustments to her care are going. In the meantime please let me know if you need anything.*

I can already hear some of you saying this is way too aggressive. I have to ask you, why do you feel that way? Do you feel that way when your dentist tells you that you have a cavity and walks you to the front desk to have their office coordinator schedule you in for a filling? The answer is probably not. The dentist understands the value of getting the cavity filled for your overall health. Do you understand the value your preventative care has on your client's overall health? We do a lot of things for our clients, and part of our work entails being a provider of preventative care. We may not be providing health screenings and blood draws to help them stay ahead of chronic illnesses, but we are providing care that prevents hospitalizations from UTIs and falls.

To help you succeed, we have provided a *Quality Assurance Form* on *The 24/7 Solution* website. This form was a key guide to help keep our Quality Assurance department on track as they evaluated a client's care and then made professional recommendations about next steps. One of the more powerful ways to ensure this document is implemented by your team members responsible for this job is to pull this document up and work on editing it together. Collaborating with your team members and lending your expertise makes for invaluable practice, and will lead to a more useful employment of the document in the home. Merely establishing this as a new expectation will make it a document that only gets checked off. Collaboration will lead to a deep understanding that the document is meant to guide them in making powerful professional recommendations that will keep seniors safe at home. Now it is time to develop yours.

24/7 SOLUTION TIME

Internal Sales

In the *Preventative Care* section of this chapter, we talked a great deal about making professional recommendations. These professional recommendations will frequently improve the hours and revenue of the business, but revenue can never be the reason for the recommendation. As we discussed in the "why-centered" chapter, the organization's core values are like guardrails, and between the mission, core values, and core purpose, you have diligently worked to make sure that your services are always driven by need and not driven by greed. It is okay to be driven to grow your hours of service and your business, but it should never come at the sacrifice of your mission and guardrails.

One of the most influential processes I ever developed in my time at Home Instead was the "Friday Forecast" meeting. While Internal Sales was a trained mindset across all team members, it was never fully and clearly understood until we began this process. "Friday Forecasts" began as a reaction to one too many losses of clients that we experienced four months into the Covid-19 pandemic. I would regularly ask my director of client care why we were losing clients, and, every time, I would hear about how someone else knew it was happening before she did and her efforts to retain these clients were coming in at the eleventh hour. While many of the losses were related to the pandemic, there were still many that were not, and our hours and revenue were being impacted. Losing one 24/7 client is bad enough, but losing multiple high-hour clients can force you to stop looking at your *Org Chart of the Future* and start looking at your Org Chart from the Past to decide who may need to go. It is not a pleasant place to land as a business owner.

After collaborating with my director of client care and continuing to peel back the layers on every loss, I developed the "Friday Forecast." It is important to remember that the time spent working with my director of client care was not a time of attack. The clients were gone, the loss had happened, and if it was clear they had made up their mind to end services, we had to move on and accept our circumstances. Shaming my director of client care for letting these losses occur because "preventing this is your job!" was a waste of time.

Instead, we dissected every case and found her excuse to be true: every single client had a story where another office team member had a tip that the loss was possibly coming and had never passed it on to her department. Many times, these tips were heard two to four weeks in advance of the phone call asking to end services – two to four weeks of precious time we could have used to salvage the relationship or educate the client on our ability to expand service offerings.

One of the details this research turned up was that it wasn't always the same team member failing to communicate. While it was often someone from our scheduling department, that was not true 100% of the time. I knew the team knew the importance of retaining clients, as well as how to be there for clients through a variety of services. So why weren't they connecting the dots? We trained on this constantly. It was tied to our mission. Their bonuses were dependent on keeping clients. Even with all of that, they would still choose to move on to their next "to do" item instead of communicating to the client care department that a primary caregiver reported their client was considering an assisted living facility.

I knew this concern was way too important to make a mere bullet item for the next weekly meeting or send another reminder email. After reflecting on the research I did with my director of client care, I came back with a very detailed process improvement plan. Moving forward, we would meet every Friday at the same time to discuss the health of the business. These meetings were not round table discussions with a vague kick-off question like, "Any concerns about losing a client?" These meetings were much more focused. It was crucial that every team member was present at these meetings. At this point in our business, we had a senior leadership team, directors, and coordinators. Regardless of their position in the company, their presence at these meetings was not only mandatory but invaluable.

Following a detailed agenda that ensured no stone was unturned, included every team member, and made sure that, every Friday, we revisited the commitments made the previous week, our offices ended up achieving the highest number of service hours ever during my last month with Home Instead. Implementing this process led to the necessary buy-in our team members needed to tie themselves back to our mission and why they showed up every day. If you are interested in implementing the "Friday Forecast" meeting using our approach, go to our website for our *Friday Forecast Implementation Guide*. It includes a step by step guide, tool, and detailed agenda you can utilize with your team.

If you scoff at the idea of an all-team meeting on a Friday, I get it. Here is what I did to overcome this challenge: I always kept it at one hour and set a timer. Everyone knew that, no matter what, we would finish within one hour. You can make it thirty minutes instead; either way, it is that many minutes of progress made to help seniors stay in their homes.

If you are not ready to implement the "Friday Forecast" meeting process, that is okay. At the very least, take the time now to determine how you can bring *all* of your team members together to retain clients. Remember, retaining clients is not just about client satisfaction; it is also about preventative care and being seen as the expert in home care.

24/7 SOLUTION TIME

Never Too Late to Retain

Every time I ask an owner "what process do you take when a client family member reports they are moving their mother into a facility?" I hear a similar version of the same story. We refer them to the facilities we trust, give them advice on how to transition smoothly, and always let them know we are there to help them however they need. My immediate reaction is to shake their shoulders, but that isn't easy to do through a computer screen – and it would probably be quite disturbing if I tried. What I appreciate about this answer is that it comes from a place of kindness and wanting to support a senior at this stage of their life. Outside of its good intentions, though, I find a lot wrong with it.

If we revisit the mission, core purpose, and core values that you wrote down in Chapter 2, I am confident most of you want to support seniors in staying home for as long as possible. I'd also be willing to bet many of you personally desire to stay home and age in place. **Yet when a family informs you they are moving their loved one, your tendency is to automatically agree.** I have a very hard time convincing owners of a mindset shift if a client loss is reported prior to my ability to teach this lesson. The reason is usually because they've already promised a family member that they will help with the transition and anything else would feel incongruent. If this describes you right now, here's my advice. As I give it to you, know that you can give this same advice to a team member one day who accidentally finds themselves in the same spot. As you reflect on your conversation and learn what the client's family member reported as the reason(s) why they are moving, reframe the scenario and say, "If a facility has the solution, why can't we provide it?"

"If a facility has the solution, why can't we provide it?"

"Mom can't shower with one caregiver anymore and needs two."

> Let's match two caregivers with your mom for four hours, two times a week to help with a shower.

"Mom's mental state has advanced so far that she won't let a caregiver help her."

> What will a facility do differently than a caregiver (or two) providing care at home? If the answer is a medical solution, why can't medical home health support your services?

"Mom is completely bedridden and cannot transfer anymore."

> How does lying in bed at a facility compare to lying in bed at home?

There are many more scenarios we have reviewed on the *Client Retention Worksheet* along with a *Home vs. Facility Cost Analysis* you can find at www.the247solution.com. This tool also provides a deep dive into how home care compares to all types of facilities, ranging from independent, assisted, skilled, group homes, to memory care units. This is a great tool to utilize with your team to kick off thinking differently about client retention.

I was mentored by a former nursing home administrator and my degree in college was for Healthcare Administration, with a focus on Nursing Home Administration. Having this knowledge and background was incredibly helpful when it came to demonstrating my expertise in home care. However, you don't need that background to do the same. As you consider the ratio of staff to patients at a nursing home, there is nothing that will compete with one-on-one care.

My spouse is a Nurse Practitioner in a medical Intensive Care Unit (ICU). Prior to being a provider, she was a nurse on that same floor for many years. The ratio of patient to nurse is two to one: one nurse for every two patients. The primary patient population in the ICU are seniors with chronic illnesses. Despite a two to one patient to nurse ratio, there are times when the hospital decides to protect certain vulnerable patients by providing a one-to-one safety sitter. Why? Because the hospital knows their nursing staff cannot be constantly present with these patients around the clock. These are patients whose health and safety are at risk due to their inability to comprehend instructions. They are likely to pull on cords, fall, and be unable to utilize the call light to ask for assistance. When a patient ends up in harm's way, the hospital is liable for this patient's health and safety.

A long-term care skilled facility doesn't have these same requirements, yet seniors still have the same needs in this setting. Even more important to point out, these seniors have a much higher patient to nurse ratio. It is not uncommon for there to be fifteen patients to one staff member, making it even worse if there is a call out and no replacement. As you look at memory care, the selling point is a smaller ratio of nurses to patients. This is true and is important. But, again, nothing can compete with the safety and quality of one-on-one care for a senior.

You are an expert in home care. I've said this before, but it's worth repeating, a lot. I would tell my team this regularly when they would find themselves nervous speaking to clients or family members about care for their loved one. They would worry or feel insecure about their knowledge because they didn't work in a nursing home or assisted living previously and weren't sure how to speak to their services. Even if my team member didn't know much about the facilities, I would instill in them that, 99.9% of the time, they know more about providing home care than any client or family member they were educating. **It is your job to stand confident in this fact and remember that their loved one can be supported at home.** If money is no object, there are only very rare occasions where being home may not be possible.

In my fourteen years of service leading franchises at Home Instead, finances aside, I came across only one scenario where I agreed a long-term care facility placement was necessary. This one memorable example was a gentleman with a special tube and machine that had to be cleaned every hour by a registered nurse. My team and I fought tooth and nail until we learned that not only was care at home not possible, finding a long-term facility for him where they had this equipment available was only possible in three facilities in the entire state. If only three skilled facilities had this, I knew I had to look at my team and agree that we were not going to be able to keep this client home.

Your client family members aren't looking to you for sympathy and support, they are looking to you for solutions.

I appreciate the home care owners' desire to approach their client family members with support when they are faced with difficult decisions like moving mom into advanced care. But I want to remind you, like I remind all of my clients, you know home care better than anyone else. Your client family members aren't looking to you for sympathy and support, they are looking to you for solutions.

One last thing: it was not uncommon for us to retain a client who had already put down a deposit at a facility. In other words, having this information is not a reason to avoid educating your client's family about the benefits of one-on-one care over a facility. If you're going to lose the client, then you might as well do all you can to convince them to stay. What do you have to lose? Before working to shift your team's mindset towards client retention, be sure to run through and become well-versed in the *Client Retention Worksheet* and *Home vs. Facility Cost Analysis*. Remember, the "24/7 Solution" starts with you.

24/7 SOLUTION TIME

9

CAREGIVER ACQUISITION

Now that we've taken a look at client acquisition and retention, it's time to move to our next pillar for a successful home care business – caregiver acquisition.

Caregiver Intake

There are a number of resources about improving caregiver acquisition on the market. I am only going to address a few points on the
topic in this book.

The approach with your "internal customers" (caregivers) is not
that different from your external customers (clients). The same care
and attention needs to be applied to your caregivers' experiences with
your company as with your clients' experiences. Gone are the days of
the stuffy HR representative.

A new favorite movie of mine is a Disney movie called *Flamin'
Hot*. This movie is the rags-to-riches story of a janitor turned executive
at Frito-Lay. In one of the scenes, Mr. Montañez is attempting to fill
out his application. The front desk clerk is less than welcoming to Mr.
Montañez and his desire to apply. In addition to treating Mr. Montañez
like an interruption to her day, her words even had an underpinning
of judgment and mockery. This wasn't unusual for the hourly worker's
experience in the 1980s, and in a lot of ways, it still isn't unusual today.

Thankfully, my experience applying as a caregiver at nineteen years
old wasn't as fraught. Many years later, I still remember my exchange
with the receptionist. She was friendly, instructed me on the next
steps while handing me a clipboard, offered me a bottle of water, and
invited me to take a seat. A year and a half later, when I was promoted
onto the administrative team, I learned that the way they captured me
as a candidate was through a weekly ad they ran in the local newspaper
on Sundays. Their recruitment department sent an email to the newspaper to get that ad placed.

In the home care industry, it is nearly guaranteed that an experience like Mr. Montañez' with Frito-Lay will result in zero caregivers
acquired with your business. But here's the even more unfortunate and
surprising reality: The experience I had when applying to be a caregiver also will not cut it anymore.

The challenge in senior care is not whether there will be any
demand for our services; the challenge is whether we'll have enough
supply. We are not the only job that applicants are considering and we
are not the only home care business. As mentioned before, I would

tease my team in times of panic to look behind them for the tiger that was chasing them. Obviously, there was never a tiger. While there is not a literal tiger chasing us, as home care providers, there is a hypothetical tiger – one that takes the form of minimal supply available. No single provider is immune to this supply and demand discrepancy; everyone is being chased by this hypothetical tiger.

As we look at this challenge facing our home care industry and try to stay a step ahead of other hourly job providers, we have to make sure we are not eaten by this tiger. The only way to survive? Run faster than everyone else! In today's market, an applicant responding to your weekly ad (newspaper or online) and receiving a warm greeting from a friendly receptionist isn't running fast enough to avoid being eaten.

Your HR team needs to have a sales mindset – more importantly, a consultative sales mindset. Every applicant is shopping the market for other hourly jobs, and if they are going to serve your clients, they need to choose yours. The best way to train your team to have this mindset can sometimes be to drop the word "sales." This word can give people the heebie-jeebies, and that is even more true for those who navigate away from the client-facing aspects of the business. If a consultative mindset still doesn't click for your team members, teach them to be educators about your company's service.

Here are a few **best practices** I always applied:

1. As stated before, mystery shop the market regularly. Beyond knowing your direct competitor's wages, know hourly employment wages across the different industries.

2. Share the pay early. Don't waste your or the applicant's time with someone looking to earn double what you can afford.

3. Inform them of your screening process early, whether you do background checks, drug screens, and so on. Make sure they know this upfront.

4. Never sound desperate. Instead, sound excited!

5. Create a pipeline for handling all inquiries to ensure your next caregiver of the year doesn't fall through the cracks before they even join the team.

6. Schedule a next step following the completion of every step. Always have the relationship and potential caregiver moving forward.

Caregiver Onboarding

As you onboard caregivers, you need to remind yourself and your team about their first day of employment with your company. Everyone has first day jitters, and, just like client families that are looking for our guidance as home care experts, caregivers need to build their confidence with the team and company from day one. We always made sure our caregivers walked into a welcoming training room. A personalized letter signed by the owner sitting on top of a branded orientation and training binder, accompanied by a name tag with lanyard, pen, and a small gift would be laid out on the table, waiting for them to arrive. As we managed in-house drug screens and Work Opportunity Tax Credit (WOTC) screening calls at the start of orientation, our caregivers were able to open their gift, read their letter, and thumb through their binder.

After completing orientation, caregivers were placed into a *Caregiver Retention Program.* We understood their first ninety days were the most crucial days in which to build trust with the company, and we wanted to stack as many cards in favor of trust being developed. As you know, building rapport with someone who rarely comes to the office is an uphill battle. To address this challenge, the *Caregiver Retention Program* would ensure we scheduled tasks to follow for every new caregiver. You can receive the full report and staff expectations on the execution of these tasks at www.the247solution.com. Below is a sample:

Sample of Caregiver Retention Program for New Caregivers:

- Introduction to first client

- First shift follow-up phone call from office

- Handwritten card from office member at two-week milestone

- Thirty-day in-office training review

Aside from the caregiver's experience on their first day (and beyond), it is important that your team remains compliant with state and federal employment laws, any home care license specific state requirements, and the standards you or your franchise has in place. Coming from someone who has been through more audits than I would like to remember, I can guarantee you that your documents are not in perfect order just because you trained your team members on what is expected. It is very easy to lose sight of what is a requirement if there isn't a system in place to protect it from being forgotten.

One of the worst moments in my career was when we did an internal audit and found a caregiver was working with our company that didn't have a background check in their file. We were huge on checklists and rarely missed anything, but this particular situation fell through the cracks. At this time, we still had paper files in-house, and the employee in charge of monitoring this process was expected to run background checks and mark them after they were complete. During the internal audit, we discovered this employee's file had everything in it except the background check from her time living in Texas. What did the checklist show? It was checked as completed. We rushed to our background check software to locate this document and hope that we had it digitally. We found it, but we discovered an even bigger problem. When we reviewed the document, right there in bright red, we saw where she had something on her background that didn't pass our normal standards. To top it off, all of this happened while I was at a conference in Florida; I had to handle it from afar.

Something important to point out here: even though they had made a series of errors, my team members still felt safe enough to call and report the errors they made. Creating a safe environment where excellence is sought after but perfection is understood as unattainable is vital to your business' success. By setting this understanding, your team knows they can trust you to work through the imperfections together with them. If your team feels like errors are unforgivable, then errors will be buried out of your sight to avoid your wrath. Errors sting, but apply the salve *together*, don't add salt to the wound. Furthermore, if your team expects punishment and rigidity versus support and solutions, errors will go unreported and unfixed.

At worst, you may be facing repercussions from your franchisor or the government without a team to support you.

Creating a safe environment where excellence is sought after but perfection is understood as unattainable is vital to your business' success.

Once we discovered the unaddressed background check and worked to make it right, we had a business decision to make. The good news is that the background check for this individual was outside of our normal standards of approval, but thankfully not against state license or franchise standards. Once we evaluated this risk, we checked with our insurance provider and learned that it would be covered should an incident ever occur with this individual. After "salving this wound" alongside the team, we were able to go back to the drawing board and figure out how we made the error. Why had we checked the background as complete without reviewing it and placing a printed copy in the employee's file? Together, and more so decided by the team member responsible for the oversight, we updated our checklist to state "run background check," added a second line to state "print background check," and a final line to say "staple to background check folder." This is how this team member chose to "salve" and prevent this "injury" in the future.

If you do not have a checklist in place (paper or digital) for onboarding requirements – from your I-9 process, to confidential information, to training requirements by the state – get one now and take your team through an internal audit. You don't have time? I understand; just know you'll have plenty of time to do an internal audit after the government or your franchise closes your doors.

24/7 SOLUTION TIME

10

CAREGIVER RETENTION

In the last chapter, we referenced the *Caregiver Retention Program* you can find on *The 24/7 Solution* webpage. While the internal audit mentioned in the last chapter is vital to keeping your doors open, this program is vital to making sure your clients are being well-served.

Unfortunately, the caregiver retention pillar is often the most neglected pillar in running a successful home care company. An interview with Dr. Aaron Blight, an international speaker and consultant on caregiving, aging, and healthcare, as well as the author of *When Caregiving Calls: Guidance as You Care for a Parent, Spouse, or Aging Relative*, enlightened me on the concept of emotional labor.

Emotional labor is the term for the concept of humans regulating their emotions for the benefit of the person in front of them. Every day, caregivers interact with a client who has unmet needs and an inability to independently meet those needs. These needs may be spiritual, emotional, physical, or mental. Providing this type of care requires frequent, sometimes even constant, emotional labor output. Unlike caregivers in facilities, one-on-one caregivers avoid long hours on their feet, unsafe conditions, and dealing with dozens of clients in a shift. However, it is difficult to quantify the toll of the emotional labor for being the sole caregiver. You are the only one available to meet the client's needs and have no external outlet for support. Dr. Blight commented, "Allowing space for caregivers to address their own mental and emotional needs is thus a critical part of leading your home care company."

There are many facets to caregiver retention that give caregivers space to address the challenges that come from the everyday exertion resultant from their emotional labor. In addition to the *Caregiver Retention Program* tool previously mentioned, we're going to hit on a few more opportunities you can create for caregivers as a home care provider.

Caregiver Training and Education

One of the most important influences you can have on retention is providing professional training for your caregivers. It is important to only promise ongoing training to caregivers that can stay within your administrative team member's bandwidth. A common mistake home care providers make is promising or requiring an ongoing training program, then failing to provide the courses. Providing online training for your caregivers is a way to prevent this, but online training is not a great way to give them the necessary space to address their own mental and emotional needs. My advice is to offer and require both online and in person.

Before I continue to discuss in person training, it is important to add that you need to know and follow the requirements of your state license. A handful of states require hands-on training to be performed by an RN, and it is often defined as a delegated task. If you do not have state requirements that require hands-on training, then my recommendation is that you raise the bar and provide hands-on training that keeps you within the realm of your state license or non-medical care services.

You may not be able to provide five different trainings a week at varying times, bring caregivers in house to work with a Hoyer lift, or teach the techniques of a sliding board transfer three times a week like you wish that you could. Instead of becoming disappointed by all that you are not doing, make a decision about what you *can* do. The first place to start is with your initial orientation and training. Determine the hands-on training components you can take everyone through at the start of their employment journey with your company.

Once your initial training is determined, create a realistic plan *with* your team on what you can do beyond the initial training. This realistic plan may be three offerings of the same training quarterly. Assuming you do not have a state or franchisor requirement saying otherwise, this is a great place to start. Don't get stuck on where you want to be in two years and let that stop you from doing something now. I often say to clients as they begin to catastrophize and overcomplicate their next steps, "You gotta start somewhere."

24/7 SOLUTION TIME

Annual Performance Evaluation

I recommend tying an annual performance evaluation to what we called an "annual refresher training." An *annual refresher training* was a smaller version of orientation and training that new caregivers completed. It tended to be the last third of orientation and training, specifically focused on the hands-on training portion. We kept it the same as the last portion of the new caregiver training so that, if we could, we would schedule annual refresher training at the same time as the new caregivers' hands-on training. This allowed our new caregivers to meet veteran caregivers and freed up time for our trainer later in the week, making it a "24/7 Solution" and not *cogging* our trainer down with the "24 hour cog" mentality. Keep in mind, we were only able to implement this approach once we had depth to our HR department. The HR manager would conduct the evaluation portion and then set the caregiver up with the trainer and new caregivers for the hands-on training portion.

Beyond the training portion of a caregiver's first year anniversary, we conducted the annual performance evaluation. In 2008, I developed an approach to evaluations that had such an impact on caregiver retention and their experiences with our company that it remained in place for the rest of my time there. I recognized the disconnect from a caregiver's experience in the home and my ability as their supervisor to have a full grasp on it. Instead of our caregivers sitting in front of a supervisor and being told how they were shaping up, I asked them to complete a self-evaluation. Prior to meeting with me, they took ten to fifteen minutes in the lobby and completed a self-evaluation form. They reported on their professionalism, ongoing professional development, work performance, and so on, and even ranked themselves on a scale of one to five. You can get a copy of the *Self-Evaluation Form* at www.the247solution.com.

While they completed that form in the lobby, I polled team members about the caregiver. I had facts in front of me, such as attendance, HR compliance, and log notes within our software, but I wanted to hear what other team members would say off the cuff. I wanted to know what was top of mind regarding this caregiver's performance. Together, the caregiver and I would work to complete their evaluation in fifteen minutes or less.

A key step in carrying out the self-evaluation piece was to always receive their evaluation before printing mine or meeting with them. By collecting their evaluation and saying I would be with them in a moment, I was able to review their perspectives and adjust my evaluation slightly, if necessary.

When it came to making adjustments, it was important to note that facts were facts and I wasn't going to sugar coat concerns that had come up about their performance. For example, if a polled team member said, "She never takes out the trash at Ms. Jones' and other caregivers have complained," and then, under the self-evaluation, the caregiver said, "Client will not let me take out trash because I am pregnant," I would change my tone in the evaluation before printing and meeting with the caregiver. Again, I never sugar-coated or shied away from addressing a topic, but I did change my posture and remembered while putting it together, "It's not what you say, it's how you say it."

During the performance evaluation, I would provide my caregiver with an appropriate pay increase and the date it would go into effect. Once I had team members doing this for the company, we would agree on a range of increase that an office staff member could give based on their evaluation.

"It's not what you say, it's how you say it."

Following the performance evaluation, the caregivers would then conduct their annual refresher training and be paid for their time in the office. If the caregiver was not able to be scheduled during the new caregiver training portion, they would still receive this training one-on-one so that they wouldn't have to return at a later date.

Prior to conducting performance evaluations annually, we would give pay increases based on hours worked. Once a caregiver had worked 1,000 hours, for example, they could get a pay increase. We learned this wasn't the best approach because it didn't consider training compliance, attendance, and so much more. Honoring these annual performance evaluations was a key part of retaining our long-term employees. If you do not have an annual performance process in place, I would get with your team and set up a "24/7 Solution" performance evaluation approach.

24/7 SOLUTION TIME

Culture of Caregiving

One of the best ways to develop a culture of caregiving is to have a career path that provides an opportunity for caregivers to potentially receive a promotion into the office. If I had not been promoted as a part-time caregiver into the office when I was a college student, you would not be reading this book right now. This opportunity for caregivers doesn't just help you find future leaders. It also helps you develop a culture of caregiving. As you promote from within, you will be onboarding administrative team members with a heart for caregiving. It is your job as their leader to encourage and ask them to also develop a heart for their work.

I have always encouraged new team members to envision a pebble being thrown into a still pond and the ripple effect it causes. Prior to their promotion into the office, you could say a caregiver acted as a worry stone for one senior at a time. While they couldn't take away their ailments, they could help them overcome their daily challenges. Now that they are in the office supporting other caregivers, they are no longer one senior's worry stone, but they are a pebble making waves of impact on the lives of many. Every time they interact with a caregiver, they are having a ripple effect on every senior cared for by these individuals and that senior's family, as well as helping more and more people stay in the comfort of their home. By promoting a caregiver into the office, you are foregoing the need to train a new hire in customer service techniques that outsiders just simply cannot understand otherwise.

In my time overseeing operations, I only had two individuals succeed in administrative roles beyond ninety days who didn't begin as caregivers. I was not against finding the best candidate for the role and always kept my options open. Based on the results, I can say today that the learning curve for embracing a culture of caregiving for someone who never worked to serve a senior was so much steeper than a caregiver's learning curve in acquiring administrative skills.

A culture of caregiving is top-down. If you are not mindfully caring for your administrative team with kindness and love, then your administrative team will not be caring for your clients and caregivers with kindness and love.

Lastly, let's not forget the caregiving you need to provide yourself. During my discussion with Dr. Blight, he reminded me that we cannot underestimate the potential impact emotional labor can have on caregivers. The same is true for you. Do not underestimate the emotional labor you have done when serving seniors, their family members, caregivers, community referral providers, and your administrative team. As the leader of the organization, your tank is potentially being emptied the most. While you treat others with kindness and love, find space to take care of your mental and emotional needs as well. We are a 24/7 business, and if we don't purposely make an effort to take a breath, we will be in a constant state of hyperventilating.

We are a 24/7 business, and if we don't purposely make an effort to take a breath, we will be in a constant state of hyperventilating.

This "24/7 Solution Time" is unlike any of the others in this book. Find space for yourself on your calendar to step away from the day-to-day of business or family obligations and refuel. See if you can schedule yourself a regular time to do something small that pulls you away from the noise. Put your phone on airplane mode and give yourself an hour to disconnect.

24/7 SOLUTION TIME

11

DEVELOPING YOUR KPIS

There is a particular story told about Warren Buffett, that his private pilot once asked him how to become successful. He recommended following the 5/25 rule. The rule is simple: identify the twenty-five most important things on your to-do list, prioritize them, and then circle the top five. Contrary to what you may think, the remaining twenty are not your secondary priorities – instead, these priorities are to be avoided at all cost. As you develop your KPIs (Key Performance Indicators), consider this sound advice by Warren Buffett.

I believe every department mentioned in Chapter 4 needs to have their top five goals explicitly stated. It is okay if it is not exactly five. Some departments may have four, and others may have six, but Buffett's advice still remains relevant: team members need their top goals and everything else needs to be avoided at all costs for at least a year.

Now is a great time to discuss the difference between a KPI and a metric for the "24/7 Solution." A KPI is always a metric, while a metric is not always a KPI. A KPI is a measurement that you are working to influence and achieve daily. In the home care world, this may be "hire four caregivers a week," whereas a metric might be "average weekly hours for each caregiver." It is very possible you may measure a metric this year and convert that metric to a KPI the following year. As you work to plan your yearly KPI goals, you may recognize your focus needs to shift to the average weekly hours for each caregiver because optimization of your caregivers is a bigger problem than the number of people starting with your organization. The choice is yours to make.

As you develop your KPIs for the organization, I do believe the owner/operator needs to have 95% of the say on where the goals should land. If you have an operational leader that allows you absentee ownership, then, together, you will want to develop the KPIs and present these to the team. We discuss this more in Chapter 12, but the point is that you should set the expectation as the leader while allowing a 5% chance to flex based on the feedback your team may provide.

Everything you need to know and accomplish in one year can be broken down into components and placed into a daily goal. Let's use a money-saving goal for example. If you have a goal to save $10,000 in one year, that is your macro goal. From there, you know that you need to save $192.31 a week, which then breaks down to $27.47 a day. I don't want to belabor this point, but this is where the breakdown often happens for home care businesses. Understanding and implementing these goals makes the difference between leading with a "24/7 Solution" mindset or a "24 hour cog" mentality.

Annual KPI Goal Setting			
Year	**Month**	**Week**	**Day**
▪ Ultimate Goal	▪ Check in on status towards annual goal accomplishment. ▪ Shift to the bigger picture. ▪ Develop a plan to overcome the bad weeks if you're not on track for the year.	▪ Is our goal on track for the week? ▪ How can I improve this week to compensate for last week's results?	▪ What do I need to do today to meet my goal? ▪ Do we need to do something extra before Friday to ensure our goal is met?
Money Savings Example			
▪ *$10,000 Saved*	▪ *I had to replace my car battery; what can I do next month to make up for the $150.00 lost from my savings?*	▪ *Have we saved $192.32 this week?*	▪ *What do I need to do tomorrow to make up for the $5.00 I didn't save towards my goal today?*
Caregiver Inquiry Example			
▪ *5200*	▪ *434*	▪ *100*	▪ *20*
Revenue Example			
▪ *$3,000,000*	▪ *$250,000*	▪ *$35,714.28*	▪ *$5,102.04*

I'd be remiss in not mentioning that the daily evaluation doesn't work perfectly for every goal. For example, revenue. Many home care organizations are serving more clients Monday through Friday than they are on Saturday and Sunday. Where this daily evaluation is most vital is in working towards the four to six KPI goals your departments are responsible for achieving. Revisiting the "home care hunter-gatherer cycle," knowing where you are in relation to these goals on a daily basis is what helps your team members maintain momentum towards their achievement.

The Home Care Hunter-Gatherer Cycle

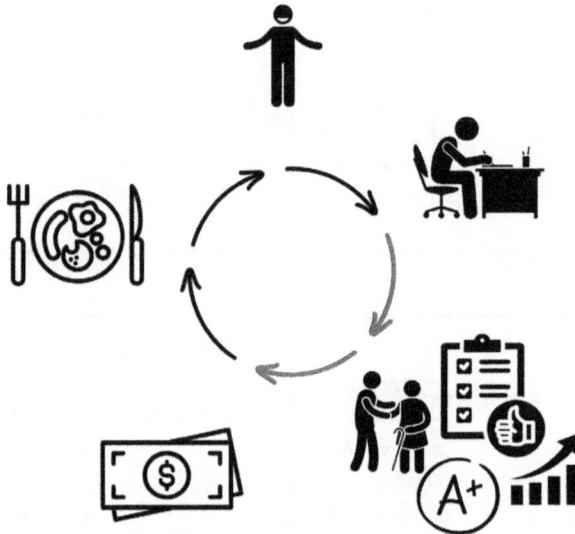

If you do not break down your KPIs into a daily measurement, represented by the lighter gray arrows in the diagram above, you risk disconnection and limit your ability to develop a fully "why-centered culture." Furthermore, momentum can be lost. Reviewing goals only from a macro perspective can remove the ability for the snowball effect to occur. Accomplishing a micro goal every day will help generate the necessary encouragement and excitement to continue accomplishing the goal; this snowball effect is what makes the macro goal possible to achieve.

Now is the time to review the KPIs and metrics in your business. Which ones need to become your goals this year? Develop four to six for each department. As the owner/operator, your main KPIs to measure are number of hours and revenue; everything else is the responsibility of your team members. We'll discuss this more in the chapter on accountability.

If you need support in developing KPIs for your organization, we do have a tool you can purchase at www.the247solution.com.

24/7 SOLUTION TIME

12

ACCOUNTABILITY

In this chapter, we are going to revisit the ways in which you will be holding your team accountable throughout day-to-day operations. We're going to begin by drawing the blueprint. As with any sturdy build, you must start by drawing up the "floor plan." This is done during your annual planning meeting. But, first, you need to find a way for your team to not only develop a plan with you, but be equally invested in the plan's success.

It is very common for owners to shy away from accountability because of the many times in their leadership during which they have been greatly challenged by team members. The primary reason accountability turns sour is when expectations are not clearly set. If you do not set expectations clearly and then hold someone accountable to an expectation they didn't understand, then and only then does "accountability" become a bad word. And guess what? You made it bad. In the book *Boundaries* by Dr. Henry Cloud & Dr. John Townsend, it states, "Problems arise when boundaries of responsibility are confused." As the leader, you are also responsible for yourself. If you are not being clear when setting expectations or outlining responsibilities, then it is not their fault they are struggling to meet them.

Bonus Structure

If your service hours goal is typically set weekly, I strongly recommend adjusting your service hours goal to a monthly goal. I also strongly discourage you from setting a bonus that is only awarded quarterly or annually based on quarterly or annual results. If you desire to offer a Christmas bonus out of kindness, you can, but the bonus we are discussing here is given based on results in hours of service. Key word, *results*. Not performance (or effort). Choosing to award bonuses to your team on their execution of their role is generous, but doesn't pay for itself. However, basing their bonus on results does.

I learned some tough lessons in my years. From starting out paying a quarterly bonus based on a certain average of revenue growth... with three tiers depending where we landed... utilizing a particular formula depending on what position they held within the company – did I lose you? Exactly. I like to use the acronym KISS - "Keep It Simple Sunshine," which I applied to many aspects of operations and most definitely in the case of pay structure and bonus opportunities.

As a business owner/operator, bonuses are not required to be paid out. As you consider base salaries for new employees, always consider their potential earnings. You can visit my website for a helpful compensation breakdown for your team members. For now, I want to speak to the winning formula for a bonus that leads to increased revenue in your business. Having this bonus structure established before getting your team to help you achieve the business' goals is very important. While we would hope the mindset of "it's what I am paid to do" would be enough to motivate better results, it's just not enough.

In the Netflix show *100 Humans: Life's Questions. Answered.* the producers bring together a hundred people from diverse backgrounds to participate in experiments. In Episode 5, "Pain vs. Pleasure," which aired March 13, 2020, the producers endeavor to answer the question regarding the better motivator. They conducted a variety of experiments. In their first experiment, it was evident that punishment had more effect in achieving results.

Before you put your bookmark here and go threaten all your employees with torture, there is more to consider. The show continues through a variety of experiments. They conducted an exercise where they evaluated the effectiveness of positive feedback versus criticism. No matter how talented or unskilled the person was, if they were provided with negative feedback, they perform more poorly on their second try. At the same time, if they were provided with praise, in making their second attempt, they outperformed their previous attempt exponentially!

Daniel Pink, best-selling author, reflected on the exercise and explained that the negative group was most likely experiencing a gap between their lived experience and what they were being told while the positive group who received praise were empowered with a sense of control.

Because our business set monthly milestones to achieve, we utilized a monthly team bonus. A team bonus was available to all administrative team members, including part-time team members, who successfully completed their ninety-day introductory period. It was that simple: if the monthly hours of service goal was met, each team member would receive a bonus equivalent to 1% of their annual salary the following month. Below is a chart displaying the formula for paying out different types of employees:

Employee Classi-fication	Salary	Monthly Bonus	Formula
Full-time	$50,000/year	$500	Annual Salary ($50,000) x 0.01 = $500
Part-time	$20.00/hour	$104	Hourly pay ($20.00) x Hours Per Week (10) x 52 weeks x 0.01 = Bonus ($104)
Per Diem	Past 90 day average earnings	$80	Past 90 Day Average Earnings ($2,000) x 4 quarters x 0.01 = x bonus ($80.00)

It is important to communicate the process of payout to your team. The chart explains how to determine the amount for the bonus. Develop a process with your finance team so they do not make mistakes. Create a system that ensures that payroll always knows whether the team met the goal for the month. Also, make sure you pay out the bonus as soon as possible. We paid our team for the 16th through the end of the month on the 10th of the following month. Paying as soon as you can and creating multiple reminders leading up to payday is a healthy way to relate to the "home care hunter-gatherer cycle" we've discussed previously. Regular reminders about what they achieved also motivates them to aim for the next bonus opportunity. I would find ways to ask team members if they had special plans for spending their bonus, or connect it back to a special goal they are trying to save money for.

Bottom line: 1% of an annual salary is affordable for your business, easy to budget, easy for your team members to understand, fair, and easy to promote.

Here are some **common mistakes** I've seen, drawn both from my own experience and those of my clients.

Setting a flat bonus for a short-term goal. In other words, announcing to your team that, if they hit a certain benchmark this month, they will get a $500.00 bonus. While that creates a temporary hype, it isn't long before one team member evaluates their work output compared to the next and realizes, "I'm doing ten times the work to achieve the goal compared to the next person, and they are going to end up earning the same reward." (Think a scheduler working to fill a 24/7 client versus a marketer getting the referral for the 24/7 client.)

Only setting bonuses for fast hits of motivation. While I do not encourage creating the expectation of bonuses being achievable in perpetuity, I do encourage setting bonuses as an expectation annually. Every year, you can reevaluate the need and remind the team that bonuses are not required. Use that stage to remind them of the choice you make as a business owner to give back to them for their results.

Setting bonuses based on performance that are not tied to revenue results. For example, establishing metrics such as number of referrals brought in versus number of closed cases with ongoing schedules.

Setting the bonus dollar amount too low. If the bonus won't even pay for a dinner for two, a movie, and a babysitter, don't do it. It won't work and will only lead to rumors that you're stingy or greedy.

Not remaining consistent. An example of this is setting a couple of bonuses based on a certain result, failing to meet the result, and then deciding to let the opportunity fizzle – meaning you never address why it failed, or that it's over.

Creating a far too complicated formula to achieve bonus. If your team member has to ask you how to get the bonus after it was announced, it's too complicated.

Tying everyone's role to the success of achieving the bonus. If anyone on your team can get the bonus while not understanding what they did to achieve it, you've failed to set the right marker. That's why in home care, the hours served goal is the only all-team bonus that ever makes sense.

Setting quarterly goals. While this shows sustained growth for the business, it removes the distance between someone's hard work and the reward. A monthly bonus is closer to the few late nights someone pulls off to make the achievement possible.

The 1% bonus takes away judgment on the dollar amount. It is possible your team members have discussed their annual salaries with one another—a habit never liked by the business owner, but that frequently happens. Nonetheless, advertising 1% removes the dollar amount by one degree and prevents team members from getting bitter, as was the case in common mistake number one.

You need to develop the monthly bonus *each month*. We learned a tough lesson by setting the bonus up for twelve months at a time. We started January with where we wanted to be and, due to a few bad months, we only achieved our bonus once that year. That will demotivate your team very quickly and make the bonus seem laughable. Instead, evaluate the next month's bonus by the 27th of the previous month. Why the 27th? For a couple of reasons. The 27th allows enough time for ensuring schedules are correct in the system, making solutions regarding pending authorizations from non-private pay clients, and it is the closest date to the start of a new month to account for any sudden major losses without you having to worry whether it falls on a weekend and you miss your chance of getting it done in time. This is the one time you, as a business owner, allow for a loss to be a reason for a lower metric. However, once that metric is set for the next month, there is no excuse for team members to not do everything in their power to achieve the goal.

Professional speaker and author Cy Wakeman stated, "The circumstances are not the reality in which you cannot succeed, they are the reality in which you must succeed." This statement sums up the shift from a "24 hour cog" to a "24/7 Solution" mindset. This theme became even better understood by my team members during Covid.

A presentation commonly requested by franchisors as a topic is my lecture on internal sales. One of the most impactful changes I made to our internal sales approach came from a weekly meeting I began with my staff titled the "Friday Forecast" (see Chapter 8 for more details). This weekly meeting's design is what took an already successful company and made it exceptional during a time of major insecurity in the world. The pandemic forced us to look in the mirror, accept our reality, and realize the situation we were in was the one in which we must succeed – not one in which we couldn't. Because of my stubbornness about not letting Covid get the best of us, my implementation of the "Friday Forecast" led to incredible results in just three months. My largest organization improved by 25% over the same time last year and I ended my career at Home Instead with this office at a record-breaking revenue since its opening in 1997. On top of that, the territory contiguous to this location grew by 16.7% over the same time, the previous year serving its second highest revenue in company history since 2007.

One of the top performing Home Instead franchisees, serving annual revenues of 7 million, reminded me of the power of my stubbornness when he posted, "The businesses Emily managed achieved double digit growth during one of the most trying times in our industry."

A monthly bonus goal versus a weekly one is important for a couple of reasons. Weekly bonuses don't show sustained growth quite as well as monthly ones. Setting a goal every week is not realistic for the already full schedule you face as an owner/operator. The ability to turn around growth by the next week feels too out of reach. A monthly goal creates just the right amount of time between when it is set and when it is accomplished. It is the sweet spot.

Additional bonuses you may want to consider.

Marketer/Business Development Bonus – An additional bonus tied to revenue from preceding month's referral sources awarded **if** the monthly bonus is met.

Internal Sales Bonus – An additional bonus tied to the individual responsible for internally selling additional hours to existing clients. This needs to be tracked and monitored very closely to ensure clients' best interests are always put first.

Overtime Reduction Bonus – If you have a problem with awarding too much overtime, tying a bonus to keeping overtime at or below a certain number may be a viable option.

Caregivers Paid Net Gain Bonus – An additional bonus tied to the individual responsible for hiring caregivers. The key to this bonus is you only pay based on caregivers being paid/working shifts. If your bonus is based on hired caregivers, you may be giving money away to an administrator who is hiring poor quality or poor availability matches for the company.

Annual Christmas Gift Bonus

Now, it is time to determine the bonus structure you want to have in your organization. Once completed, be sure to announce this to your team and utilize it as daily motivation to help your organization achieve its goals.

24/7 SOLUTION TIME

Annual Planning Meeting

An annual planning meeting takes place every year. It is very important that the owner is a part of this once-a-year meeting. Many owners say "I don't have time" as they rush to meet with a family for care and back to the office to clean up a mess made by a scheduler. The reality is, you don't have time not to! This annual planning meeting is the key to a successful year for your business. Yes, things will still get in your way, and you may have turnover from a key team member by the time next year is over, but that doesn't take away from the crucial nature of this meeting for your business.

Before reading on, it's important to define a few key words from the agenda soon to follow:

Key Performance Indicator (KPI) – These are the items you have defined as important metrics in your business to measure, track, and establish goals to hit. Often, KPI is used synonymously with "goal."

Metric – These are the data points in your business that are important to measure and track, but that are not necessarily pivotal enough data points to have as a goal.

Goal – This is the number for the KPI you are measuring. For example, if you have decided your business needs to hire four caregivers a week to grow, the goal is then four. Keep in mind, "goal" in this context is not lofty or overly optimistic, it is the *expectation*. These numbers are inflexible for the year you are planning. "Goal" is often synonymous with KPI.

Tactic – This is the technique you will apply to achieve the goal. Tactics are intended to be flexible, but not fluid. *Flexible* is pivoting after thorough evaluation, whereas *fluid* may be changed on a daily basis and allow for emotions to be in the driver's seat of the change.

Playbook – This is a working document that details how you will achieve your goals. This includes everything beyond processes.

Process – A process is how you complete a task. For example, the step by step guide you would often see in a user's manual explains a process.

You can find a detailed *Annual Planning Meeting Agenda* on *The 24/7 Solution* website.

The annual planning meeting sets the stage for the entire year. The sample agenda we provide is an outline for a leader who already has a set accountability structure in place. If accountability is a new concept for your team, it's important to carve out a one- to two-hour section to clearly define the accountability structure they can expect moving forward. Over the next few sections, I will identify the structures you will want to use with your teams.

Here's the thing: the only way this works, and the needle is moved, is if you commit as the leader. You must model the expectation you have for your team. A common issue with my clients is that "they did that and it didn't work." When I dig deeper into what they mean, I always learn that they stopped doing it within three months because they had things come up. As the owner/operational leader, if you want to have freedom 90% of the time and the ability to work *on* your business as opposed to merely *in* your business, you have to commit to the accountability structure and show up. Don't cancel. Reschedule if you must, but *always* show up. If you can push through the desire to cancel, I promise you, your business will flourish versus suffer. In terms of building a house, this accountability structure is the four walls. If you don't put the four walls up and then try to hang a picture you will realize quickly you do not have anywhere to hang your picture.

Monthly Accountability Meeting

Now that you have scheduled these meetings for the upcoming year, it's time to show up. These meetings with your team need to be seen as sacred. If you do this as the owner/operator, your team will consider these meetings just as crucial to carry out with their direct reports. This is how you scale; this is how your forty-hour work week compounds into the effects of multiple forty-hour leaders. As the owner/operator, it is very important to always come prepared. There are ways to come to the table too prepared and not prepared enough. In my experience, I can think of a handful of times where I over-prepared for my meeting with a team member and then, when we kicked off, they dropped a bomb in my lap. Sometimes that bomb was a letter of resignation; sometimes that bomb was a conflict in their schedule that contradicted my plans for them. All the work I did to prepare was quickly thrown away. What I learned to do instead was follow a template. My website has a sample monthly accountability meeting template to help set your accountability meetings up for success.

Within this template, you will find a section for reviewing KPIs. The way I always describe a perfect accountability meeting is this – your direct report arrives, provides you a report of the KPIs since the last meeting, and then explains the successes they had and why, along with their plan to maintain them. Next, they report about their opportunities, where they didn't meet their goals, and their plans regarding what they will do to improve the results by the next meeting. In this time, they may bring up a desire to adjust a tactic that was developed previously. When addressing this desire, they need to be very clear about the data that supports this change. Once the data is presented and the case is made, they need to let you know their replacement plan: "Instead of 'x,' I'm now going to do 'y' in order to achieve this goal." This change will need to be very thorough and measurable. Once they've made their case for this change and all metrics have been reviewed, you are able to simply say "Thank you."

The key here is that you didn't say a word the entire time they presented; they provided you with such a detailed presentation on addressing their successes and opportunities with KPIs that you couldn't find any holes to poke in their plans. As I teach this to clients, I always remind them that this would be a utopic accountability meeting and isn't realistic. However, what is realistic is expecting your team members to come to you prepared and ready to celebrate their successes, able to identify where the credit for the successes belongs and defend their choices to make changes to tactics. As their supervisor, you need to spend that time challenging different angles and making sure they do not have any blind spots. Your collaboration with your team member in these meetings is the one-degree difference you need to get from really hot water to boiling water!

Sam Parker says it best in his book *212° The Extra Degree*, "211° can serve a purpose, but 212° is the extra degree – the extra degree that will bring exponential results." Your team member comes with 211°, a majority of the work completed. Your effort is just a single degree addition that leads to the business' success. So often, even the best-run offices fall prey to owners doing 211° of the work, with the team members doing only the final degree. If this is you, this accountability process is one of the most powerful shifts you can make in your business that leads to a "24/7 Solution."

It is very important that you have a record of what was agreed upon during your meeting with your team member. Having a meeting where nothing is put in writing, especially in the ever-changing world of a home care business, is equivalent to not having a meeting at all. You can send an email or type notes in a Word document; we always kept a Word document of meeting minutes because it wasn't uncommon for us to want to use special tables and charts to make a record of our results.

One of the most efficient and effective changes I made to my accountability meetings with team members was a simple shift in how we ended up with accountability meeting minutes. For many years, I would meet with my team and take notes, make agreements, and then, after the meeting was over, type up a Word document and email it to them. I had convinced myself that the time redigesting the information and typing it later helped me better solidify the action items into my memory bank.

A few things would happen when I managed it this way. One, I tended to forget what a note meant. I would go to my direct report and seek clarification and, at times, we would both fail to remember what we had previously found to be very important. Ah, the workings of a 24/7 home care business. Second, I would find much more important and urgent matters to handle with my team. As soon as we would dismiss, another team member was knocking on my door to ask about a new long term care client's paperwork or to let me know there was an issue with parking and the landlord was there to discuss it. The scribbled notes would sit on my desk until the urgent matters were managed. Sometimes, that meant they sat for days. Despite my desire to do better, I would inevitably have to choose an urgent matter over the important matter of minutes. Lastly, time would pass, and then I would finally send the minutes to my team member. They would land in their inbox and be filed away until my team member could get back into the headspace of what we had discussed. A week would go by, and they would finally review them and find themselves confused by what we agreed upon in a few of the bullet points and then try to find a good time to meet with me to review and get clarification. At best, we are now one to two weeks out from our monthly meeting. A month only has four or five weeks. Essentially, we'd meet to plan a month's action steps and, halfway through the month, still be plotting our implementation of many of the items we discussed. It was maddening.

As is often the case in business and in life, I had a "light bulb moment" and realized how to make this process work better. Instead of losing two weeks of productivity, accruing frustrated mental energy with myself and my team members and delayed time trying to remember what we meant, I began typing minutes during our time together. I was never more thankful for my grandmother teaching me how to type on her typewriter as a child than I was when I figured out this hack. While in the meeting, I would share my screen and type exactly what we were agreeing to; furthermore, I would gut the previous month's minutes and use them to keep us on track and make sure none of the old agenda items fell through the cracks.

Here is an example of a tactic around hiring caregivers that we would evaluate during our monthly accountability meetings.

Tactic Example	Quality of Tactic on a 5 Star Scale
Recruit caregivers online.	★
Place ads on findajob.com.	★★
Place an ad every Monday, Wednesday, and Friday on findajob.com.	★★★
Place an ad every Monday in the metro area with a general need for caregivers, every Wednesday for specific cases such as — "'x' location, twelve-hour days," and place an on Fridays for retirees interested in giving back on findajob.com.	★★★★

Place an ad every Monday in the metro area with a general need for caregivers, every Wednesday for specific cases such as – "'x' location, twelve-hour days," place an on Fridays for retirees interested in giving back on findajob.com. Evaluate the results for each ad weekly, paying particular attention to the number of inquiries, interviews, hired caregivers, and number of start dates. Utilize this data to better understand which ads lead to start dates from new hires versus quantity of inquiries. Do this consistently for three months. In the event that more needs beyond what this covers arises within our company, we will post additional ads at that time.

★ ★ ★ ★ ★

It is very important to remember that your role as the supervisor is to evaluate hiring tactics for specificity and action that can be measured. A common goal may be to improve caregiver retention and a possible tactic may be to "love on" caregivers. This is not specific or measurable. But "loving on" caregivers can be accomplished through specific and measurable actions – perhaps calling one caregiver a week to check on them, writing one thank you note a week to an unsuspecting caregiver, sending birthday cards to caregivers, and so on.

As noted on the template provided on my website, it's important to always end each meeting with two very important things. The first is easy if the annual planning meeting has been executed correctly – confirm the next accountability meeting date and time. Making sure this time is on the calendar and considered sacred is key to moving the needle in your business. Revisiting it during this meeting ensures there are no issues with upcoming vacations/holidays/urgent business and resets the target that all the previously discussed action items have a deadline for achievement.

Next, always finish each meeting as the supervisor with, "Is there anything you need from me to help make your job easier and more successful?" In my years of leading monthly meetings, I rarely forgot this closing. When I did, I always regretted it. Inevitably, if I failed to ask this question, I would learn fairly quickly of an issue that was challenging my team member that just didn't seem to come up for them based on the metrics and, yet, it would make their results and the business suffer. More importantly, this question provided an opportunity to connect with my team members beyond the professional walls we met within. They would usually answer "no," but go on to share that their daughter just started piano lessons, that they were looking to buy a new home, that they were saving for braces for their oldest. Many took this question into the realm of personal matters. Learning their life goals always helped me lead them and empower them to succeed in their role. If I knew they had a goal of buying a new house, I wouldn't think twice about their last-minute request to see a house that just went on the market in hopes to capture it before someone else did. If I knew they were saving for braces, I could start saying "momma needs a new pair of braces" when we would discuss how close we were to achieving the monthly team bonus. This easy but important question is what helped me develop relationships with my team members that carried them in their careers at my company long past the typical turnover rate of the average home care business administrative team member.

Two **Must Do's** at the End of Every Accountability Meeting

1. Confirm the next accountability meeting date and time.

2. Ask, "Is there anything you need from me to help make your job easier – and you more successful?"

As you read this, you may be saying, "I already know all of that about my team members!" My response to that is that I'm cautiously glad that you do. In the years of acquiring existing home care businesses, more times than not, the owner was not hated by their team. In reality, most every owner was met with tears upon the announcement of their retirement/selling of the business. The team members loved the owners. However, the team members did not necessarily respect them as business leaders. Knowing all the personal goals of your team members is powerful, but if your time spent interacting with your team is 70% about their personal goals, 20% about their complaints with caregivers/challenges in the business (problems), and 10% about what they are going to do to make things better (solutions), your leadership is misguided. Are you wanting to be their life coach or their business leader?

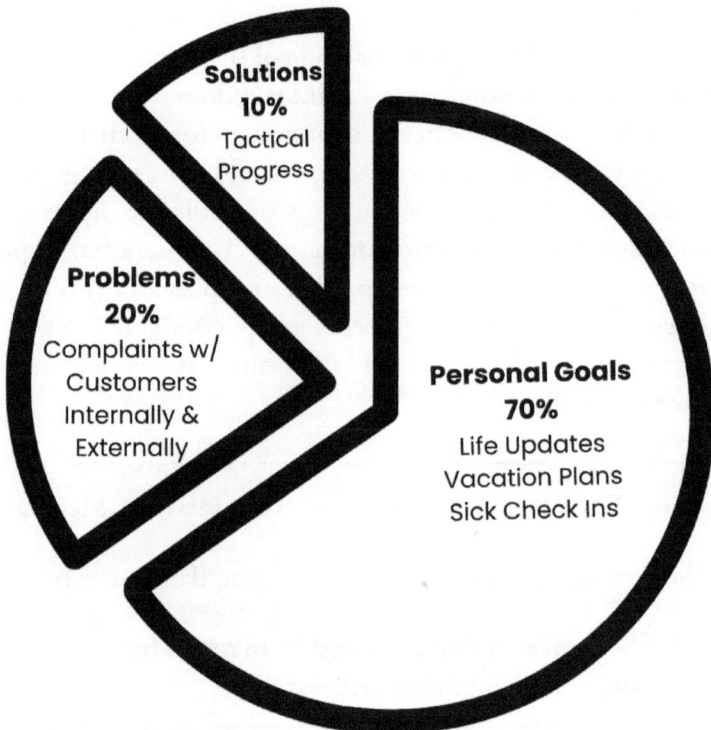

To this day, I have great relationships with my past team members. Two of my past team members sought me out after they ended their roles in the businesses I had built and asked to work for me again. Others, I hear from because of leadership quotes that reminded them of me, others ask to have dinner to catch up, and one insists on babysitting. I loved my team members; however, I respected them and they respected me. I showed them respect by holding them to the standards expected of them in their profession. Our professional relationship came first, but never did it trump what they meant to me as human beings and contributors in this world.

Our interactions were more likely to carry out in this manner.

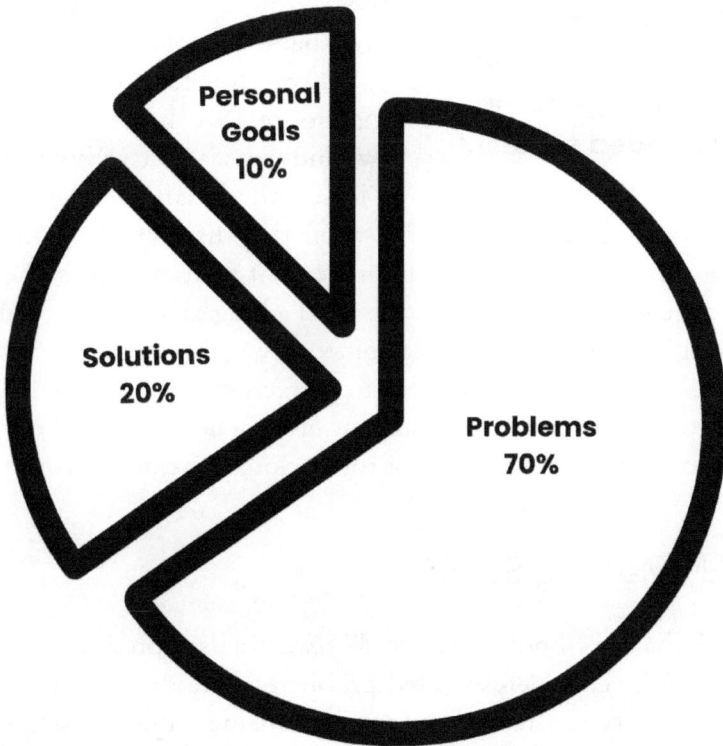

Unfortunately, the second question, "Is there anything you need from me to help make your job easier – and you more successful?" sometimes led to words I didn't want to hear. We would finish their meeting, and I would ask that question and learn that they were looking to move to a different state in the next three to six months because their spouse was going to be transferred. I would learn they were looking for a new job because, although they loved so much about what they did, there were too many obstacles standing in their way of their desire to stay. Question number two didn't always give me what I wanted to hear, but it always gave me what I needed to hear. Because of that question, I opened the door for a team member to work with me through their departure, work with me to find a way to cater to their skills and stay on board, or provide them a listening ear to help them grow as a professional, however that may look.

Question number two didn't always give me what I wanted to hear, but it always gave me what I needed to hear.

In my fourteen years of leading home care businesses, I had two individuals quit without notice. Those individuals' sudden departures weren't entirely surprising when they happened. Both were working through performance improvement plans and, as some may say, saw the writing on the wall. I learned a long time ago that individuals are either a hiring mistake or someone who has not been properly coached. You cannot hire or coach to perfection, but, as I often tell my clients, you can stack the cards in your favor. These monthly meetings and this one question will do a lot for stacking the cards in your favor.

Weekly Meeting Structure

Patrick Lencioni's book, *Death by Meeting*, focuses on a cure for the most painful, yet underestimated problem of modern business: bad meetings. There is a reason the internet meme, "this meeting could have been an email" became so popular. There is a right dose of meetings for every business, and in every industry, that dose is different. For home care operation, the following frequency is best:

Type	Frequency
One on One w/supervisor	Monthly and as needed
One on One w/peer	As needed
Leadership Team Meeting	Weekly (Monday mornings)
All Team Meeting	Weekly (Friday Forecast – See *Internal Sales* section for more details)

For many years, I would have my leaders sit with me at 9:30 a.m. every Monday and rattle off their metrics. As they sat with me and spoke to their results, even as the leader, I would almost fall asleep. When I was awake, however, I would catch concerns and bring them up to the team members in the room. For instance, if my marketer said they only asked five referral sources for business during the previous forty-hour work week, I was quick to pause and dig into why. It served as a great avenue for peer accountability, but I was always forced to walk a fine line between what should be handled as a team versus what should be handled with someone privately regarding their performance – oftentimes crossing the line. With the setup I had in place, at worst, I was publicly shaming a team member about a metric they didn't meet in front of team members who had zero insight on how to help. At best, I was wasting precious labor hours of my team members as I sat and spoke over their heads about their teammates' metrics. This went on for over ten years, with the justification that it was the one time a week we came together as a team and this time together was invaluable.

In 2016, I began overseeing two organizations with two separate leadership teams. Suddenly, I had to figure out a way to do what I had been doing for a more than forty hour job of directly leading one home care business serving 2500 hours/week in care in only *twenty* hours – for two businesses! I didn't have an hour and a half to hear metrics rattled off and write them in my notebook, only to do it again next week. I was sitting in one office in the morning and another office that afternoon, carrying out a meeting to set the stage for the week for two different home care businesses twenty-five miles apart. I couldn't afford to clutter my mind with data from reports that had zero action.

In addition, we would spend every Monday going over the on-call report verbatim. It was standard for us to have our on-call supervisor keep a time journal of every call that came in and to ensure it had enough detail to prevent any unanswered questions. This process, depending on the incidents over the weekend, would take sixty to ninety minutes, just spent reading and processing the information with the team. Again, this was justified for years as a way to ensure no communication was dropped between Friday and Monday, and that our clients received the same quality of care regardless of the day of the week. Sounds noble, right? Here's the thing: we all didn't need to know that Susie called on Saturday night asking how to bake a sweet potato for Mr. Smith. We didn't need to know that Josie was struggling to find the right house, but the on-call supervisor directed them to the client's home without a problem. How were either of those going to help us hire more caregivers or obtain more referrals? They weren't.

It was then that I decided things had to be more efficient. In some ways, I had to let go and trust my leaders, and, in other ways, I had to find a way to get the same information without letting go but while respecting my other team members' time. I began having the team submit their metrics in a spreadsheet ahead of our time together. In addition to them submitting their metrics, it was *their* job to point out red flags *and* provide a plan of correction to present to the team. I would then review that information quickly, approximately fifteen minutes before the meeting, and make note of any red flags that I noticed and prepare to address with the team as a whole. My hope was that they would see the same red flags and be ready with a plan to correct them.

More often than not, that was the case; however, this exercise, which required them to prepare and present without notifying me in advance, allowed us to find more opportunities for improvement together. If I noticed a red flag that they didn't provide a plan for, we would use the time together as a team to dive in, or decide during the meeting to set up a follow-up one on one meeting. The adage "two brains are better than one" came into play here, and my not knowing their plan of correction in advance decreased the likelihood that I would just agree with their ideas. Instead, my perspective on the topic may have uncovered more issues that they were not seeing.

In regards to the on-call report, reviewing this was still very important. Reviewing it all together? Not so much. Instead of every journal entry being reported, it became the job of the scheduler to review the on-call report first thing every morning, highlight the matters that impacted scheduling, client care, community reputation, and HR, and report only those highlighted matters. Some weeks we still spent thirty to forty-five minutes processing the report; however, this time was spent developing a tangible action plan to make a particular situation right. Did a caregiver smoke in a non-smoking zone at a SNF? Let's deploy our marketer there immediately and have HR contact the caregiver to provide correction. Did a caregiver fail to show at a client's place because they spent over an hour looking for the home and gave up? Let's get the person who did the consultation to write detailed instructions in the system on how to find the home, or, better yet, let's agree that the client needs to always have an office representative meet the caregiver at the convenience store down the street from the home and let them shadow them to the house. Instead of falling asleep to status updates on late notifications and random questions about how to use a client's stove, our leaders were focusing on what mattered to each other and to the seniors and caregivers in our care.

Furthermore, we weren't spending our time reading off numbers that meant nothing to most of the team. Instead, we were spending roughly an hour focusing on the items that would move the needle for the business. Beyond that, we were engaging our peers in solving the issues we were having, looking for outside-the-box ideas. Could the marketer have some experience related to a problem we're having with a recruitment matter? Could a scheduler help brainstorm some marketing messages based on the caregiver pool that is ready to work? Does the quality assurance leader have suggestions on mapping and managing time to accomplish in person visits for the marketer?

We finally distilled these meetings down to what mattered most and getting rid of the environment of judgment that arose from putting people in the hot seat.

Don't get me wrong, the seat was still hot. There is incredible power in peers sitting in a room with one another, discussing their biggest challenges transparently and vulnerably. The difference is the responsibility shifted to each individual in that room, not just me. It required everyone to come prepared, and, if you didn't and everyone else did, the discomfort of shirking one's accountability was palpable without the leader even saying a word. Beyond that, the team members came with well-thought-out plans, not haphazard, off-the-cuff ideas. Even if the team member prepared their plan at 9:15 a.m., fifteen minutes before the meeting, they still took time they didn't take previously to prepare to present their solution to the red flags in their report. Not only did they prepare, they prepared their *solution*. Gone were the days when schedulers could come into the meeting and say, "I need more caregivers." If they noticed that their ratio of caregivers to clients were increasing, they were evaluating why and providing data to support their case. If, in fact, it was because they needed more caregivers they could specifically state, "I need more caregivers in ABC Town for eight-hour shifts with a bedridden client because this client saw five different caregivers last week." Through this solution and collaboration with regard to recruiting, other team members heard the plan, and agreement occurred between peers while I sat and took notes. That's it. I had found a way to develop leaders within the organization and multiply my efforts simply by setting them up with an expectation to prepare and report differently.

Another important piece of this meeting is that I prepared for it by looking at the business' future. In these meetings, it was important that I set the company's vision for the next four to eight weeks. It would take all week for me to prepare for these meetings. Sounds daunting, huh? It was actually very easy. Throughout the week, items would come across my radar that the team needed to learn about. In a lot of cases, leadership development topics would come across my deck that inspired me, and I knew they would inspire my team as well. Instead of spending two or three hours on Sunday night trying to scan through things that I needed to report, I would update my calendar with a note. All week long, I would return to my weekly appointment that was upcoming and make a note of an item I needed to speak to the team about. Instead of dedicating chunks of Sunday night or early Monday morning to preparing, I would review my prompts and distill them down to a finalized agenda. Many times, what I thought was important last Tuesday would be shifted to the following week and another item would take priority.

As referenced in the *Weekly Meeting* template on *The 24/7 Solution* website, every meeting started with a five to thirty minute kickoff by me. It was my job to notice the red flags in everyone's reports and evaluate the amount of time we may need to spend with each team members' burning issues. Once I evaluated those items, I would then pick the items that had to be addressed. For example, if, in three weeks, we have our quarterly caregiver meeting, we should finalize the agenda today. Then there were items that could be postponed, like a ten-minute Ted Talk to inspire time management. For the items that could wait, I would move them to the following Monday's weekly meeting. My goal was to always ensure we were participating in meetings with items that mattered most to everyone.

Because of this shift in the weekly meeting process, I was able to grow two offices while only being able to work part-time hours for each office. Specifically, my initial office grew by 21.6% in the first two months of splitting my time, and my second territory grew 200% by the twelfth month! Finding a way to more efficiently lead two leadership teams during a Monday meeting was the key to this success. Why Mondays? My mentor at the time made it clear to me that kicking a week off on the right foot made the difference between a winning week and a losing one.

Empowering your leaders to lead through coaching is one thing; setting up templates and expectations for them to follow elevates them to an entirely different level.

Empowering your leaders to lead through coaching is one thing; setting up templates and expectations for them to follow elevates them to an entirely different level.

End of Day Reporting

We began the *Accountability* chapter with a macro view of how to set the stage for accountability throughout the year. As we continued to walk through the accountability structure for your team, we dove deeper and deeper into a more micro view. One of the most pushed-against steps from my clients is end of day reporting. There is a litany of reasons why this creates hesitancies for owners. Here are common oppositions:

1. It's micromanagement.
2. It won't be done.
3. The team doesn't have time to do that on top of everything else.
4. If you hire professionals, you shouldn't need this.
5. I don't need this information daily as long as it's getting done.

You've likely heard this before: "what gets measured gets managed." Peter Drucker, management guru, continues on to say " – even when it's pointless to measure and manage it."

What Drucker is saying here is that organizations can swing the pendulum too far the other way – having administrative team members report on every metric possible to the point that their weekly report is a six-page document. Now that we recognize that the micro step is end of day reports, it's even more important to focus on measuring what really matters.

As Drucker says, expecting numbers to be reported "even if it harms the purpose of the organization to do so" is a common trap leaders fall into. For example, if you need to hire five caregivers a week, you may be tempted to have individuals report daily on each metric, from inquiring to hiring. While these metrics are valuable and need to be reviewed for trends, perhaps monthly, the most pivotal piece in the funnel is what you would want to focus your team members on for end of day reports. Perhaps having your team member report the number of applications, number of interviews conducted, and number of caregivers hired is all you need in a daily report. An incessant number of metrics to report on might consist of: inquiries; conversion percentage of inquiries to applicants; applicants; conversion percentage of applicants to interviews; interviews scheduled; conversion percentage of interviews scheduled to conducted; interviews conducted; conversion percentage of interviews conducted to job offers made; so on and so forth. After typing out that list of metrics, I can see why Drucker's full quote references the harm overreporting can cause for a business and their employees.

You cannot and are not asking your team to report an end of day for the sake of reporting. Instead, you're asking them to measure for the sake of managing. The most powerful part of the end of day report is the "plan to improve results" section. In this section, you are asking your team member to give a moment of their time to think about where their measurements line up in relation to their goal. If a scheduler has a goal to keep overtime hours at less than twenty hours a week, but they report on Tuesday they are at twenty-five, this is a problem.

The *End of Day* template you can find on my website, when honored by your team member, will require your team member to acknowledge their status on goal and their plan to meet the goal. In other words, under the section "plan to improve results," they may say, "Contact Mr. Smith and explain that we will not be able to have Susie there this week due to overtime. Find out if Mr. Smith desires a different caregiver or would rather pay a premium fee to keep Susie in the shift." Using this example, let's discuss the common objections and how I address these objections with my clients.

It's micromanagement.

Micromanagement is having a mindset of "control every part, however small, of an activity." The above example does not involve controlling a team member. It is simply providing the infrastructure and an expectation for them to report to you how they will meet their goals.

It won't be done.

It won't be done if you allow it to be missed. What gets permitted gets promoted. It is your responsibility to make this second nature for your team members. I often use the restaurant industry as an example: anyone who has been a server knows they cannot leave their shift until the salt shakers are refilled and the silverware is rolled. This end of day report must become their version of rolling silverware. They cannot leave until it's done, and if they do, there will be consequences. In the case of home care, the consequence simply has to be a text requesting their end of day, and after two to four weeks of this consistency to ensure it is done, your team member will have the habit in place. In addition to consequences, acknowledgements and engagement with their report when sent is also a key way to positively reinforce the habit.

The team doesn't have time to do that on top of everything else.

Let's go back to the "24 hour cog" mentality; if you do not ask your team to bookend their day with an end of day report, then you are not asking them to start their next day with a plan. If you do not ask them to start their next day with a plan, then you're encouraging them to remain stuck in the "24 hour cog" mentality. Now overtime is at forty hours that week, as opposed to twenty-five, and there is zero awareness of how far from the goal your team member is until it is too late.

If you hire professionals, you shouldn't need this.

In the beginning of this book, we discussed the practice of debriefing. As I think about the most professional and respected industry where mistakes simply are not allowed, these professionals have a very thorough debrief practice. It's not rocket science, but I guarantee you rocket scientists are completing their own version of a measurement-tracking system similar to an end of day. In our example, the end of day report acts as a checklist, a measuring tool, a planning tool, a reporting tool, and it forces a debrief of your team members' days.

I don't need this information daily as long as it's getting done.

Even the most excellent among us are not perfect. If it's not getting done today, when is it going to be? Four days too late?

Getting to this micro level of measurement and planning is what will lead to the accomplishment of your macro goals. For those with bonus structures in place, your team members will be motivated to keep track daily and know where they stand in hopes of achieving the business' macro goals.

Now it is time to pull everything together from the *Accountability* chapter and implement expectations with your team. Reviewing all that this chapter entailed is key to successful implementation. Now that you have a grasp on the bigger picture, it is time to go back to the beginning of this chapter and determine the best implementation plan for your business. If you are not sure where to start, you can reach out to us at www.the247solution.com.

24/7 SOLUTION TIME

CONCLUSION:
YOU HAVE NOT ARRIVED

The entrepreneurial story is a journey; you never "arrive." This is even more true for home care. Every day is a new day, and brings with it a new set of obstacles and risks for your organization. You have come a long way since beginning this book and made incredible strides to support your business' operations and scalability. All of your hard work and system development is just the beginning of your home care story.

The "24/7 Solution" begins with developing a "why-centered culture" that reminds everyone *why* they joined your organization, including yourself.

The "24/7 Solution" requires your attention and intention in developing systems that lead your team members to have autonomy while also holding them accountable. While the meeting structure and reports push your teams a great deal, you must still inspect their results regularly. You cannot be afraid to get into the weeds with your team members. A common mistake my clients make is believing they can set it and forget it. This mindset is the equivalent of buying a treadmill and thinking you will get into shape. Many things have to come into play before you get in shape. Then, once you do get in shape, you cannot unplug the machine and simply be able to stay in shape.

The "24/7 Solution" requires you to embrace empathy over excuses. Once you have set the foundation, which includes consistent reporting and management of metrics, and you provide frequent inspection of the results, then you must embrace empathy over excuses. Excuses are relevant to navigating next steps, but they are not reasons you cannot succeed. Recognize the reality, be empathetic about the situation, and work *together* to find a solution.

Excuses are relevant to navigating next steps, but they are not reasons you cannot succeed.

You have embarked on a journey that will have an incredible impact. You have the privilege to provide jobs in your community *and to* provide an incredible service to seniors and their families. This work is not easy; in fact, it can be very difficult at times. The "24/7 Solutions" you are implementing today will help you make an impact on those in your community for years to come.

As I conclude this book, I must remind you, as I was once reminded, "There is no other business where you have the opportunity to earn such an incredible income, provide incredible jobs, and serve seniors the way we have here." Furthermore, there are very few industries that exist today that give the level of job security the senior home care industry provides.

If you are ever in need of support and encouragement to continue another day, I encourage you to return to this book.

If you are ever in need of additional support and encouragement, or you're at the point of closing up or selling your business because of your inability to scale, due to challenges with turnover, inability to find time with your family, a failure to earn the profits you had hoped you would earn, or any other reason – please reach out to us at www.eiandcompany.com. We would be honored to help you in your journey. Who knows? Maybe that one step will make all the difference between you being the struggling owner of one business today and the thriving owner of seven businesses in five years, or the difference between serving 200,000 hours of care to seniors this year and 1 million hours of exceptional care in five years.

REVIEW INQUIRY

Hey, it's Emily here.

I hope you've enjoyed the book, finding it both useful and motivational. I have a favor to ask you.

Would you consider giving it a rating wherever you bought the book? Online book stores are more likely to promote a book when they feel good about its content, and reader reviews are a great barometer for a book's quality.

So please go to the website of wherever you bought the book, search for my name and the book title, and leave a review. If able, perhaps consider adding a picture of you holding the book. That increases the likelihood your review will be accepted!

Many thanks in advance,

Emily Isbell

WILL YOU SHARE THE LOVE?

Get this book for a friend, associate, or family member!

If you have found this book valuable and know others who would find it useful, consider buying them a copy as a gift. Special bulk discounts are available if you would like your whole team or organization to benefit from reading this. Just contact us at support@the247solution.com.

WOULD YOU LIKE EMILY ISBELL TO SPEAK TO YOUR ORGANIZATION?

Book Emily Now!

Emily Isbell accepts a limited number of speaking engagements each year. To learn how you can bring her message to your organization, email support@the247solution.com or visit www.eiandcompany.com.

GLOSSARY

ADL (Activities of Daily Living): Activities related to personal care. They include bathing or showering, dressing, getting in and out of bed or a chair, walking, using the toilet, and eating.

Admin Percentage: The percentage of administrative salaries to revenue in the same measuring period.

Aging in Place: The idea of staying in your own home as you become older.

EVV (Electronic Visit Verification): A term used in home care to describe the technology used to track a caregiver's arrival and departure from a client's home.

Goal: This is the number for the KPI you are measuring. For example, if you have decided your business needs to hire four caregivers a week to grow, the goal is then four . Keep in mind, "goal," in this context, is not lofty or hopeful – it is the *expectation*. These numbers are inflexible for the year you are planning.

Gross Margin: The gross profit as a percentage of revenue. Gross margin helps a company assess the profitability of its services.

KPI (Key Performance Indicator): These are the items you have defined as important metrics in your business to measure, track and establish goals to hit.

Marketing: Marketing includes sales, while sales does not include marketing. Marketing is about the overall brand recognition within your community. Your marketer may be responsible for this in your business or it may be shared with the owner. However, your marketer is 100% responsible for the sales of receiving referrals from the community.

Metric: These are the data points in your business that are important to measure and track but are not necessarily pivotal enough data points to have a goal.

No Call, No Show: A common term used to describe a caregiver failing to communicate their absence and failing to show for a shift.

Playbook: This is a working document of how you will achieve your goals. This includes everything beyond processes.

Process: A process is how you complete a task. The step by step guide you would often see in a user's manual.

Profit Margin: The percentage of revenue the owner can draw from the business.

Stakeholders: Anyone with an interest in or concern associated with your home care business. These are most often clients, client family members, caregivers, administrative team members, and referral providers.

Tactic: This refers to the technique you will apply to achieve your goal. Tactics are intended to be flexible – but not fluid. "Flexible" means pivoting after thorough evaluation, whereas "fluid" refers to that which may change on a daily basis and allow for emotions to be in the driver seat of the change.

Telephony: A term in home care used to describe the tracking of caregivers' arrival and departure from a client's home. Similar to EVV.

Trim Goals: A goal that is set with an understanding that accomplishing less as the business grows is expected.

Veteran Caregivers: A term we regularly used to delineate between new caregivers, those in their first ninety days and veteran caregivers, and anyone with our organization more than ninety days.

Work Opportunity Tax Credit: A tax credit available to employers for hiring individuals from targeted groups who have faced barriers to employment. Your payroll provider should be able to help you find out if you qualify.

ABOUT THE AUTHOR

Prior to Emily Isbell's departure from Home Instead, she implemented scalable systems that led to seven units across rural and metro territories in three different states. Annual revenues totaled $20.4 million in 2020 with 17 million or more of those revenues coming from private pay clients.

Emily began her home care career with Home Instead in Bowling Green, KY in 2007 as a caregiver. Within five years, she worked her way up to second-in-command. Her leadership doubled the number of caregivers on staff and improved the turnover percentage from 151.8% to 56.5%. Knowing the 2008 recession was on the horizon, she developed programs to increase efficiency in all departments – growing hours of service to 19,500 hours/month in spite of the economic challenges the nation was facing. This placed their franchise as third out of roughly 550 franchise units at the time. From there she went on to become the face of multiple units and allowed the owner to remain out of the day-to-day operations. Growing businesses every step of the way, her most notable achievements growing one organization by 434% in four years and another by 200% in just one year.

Today, Emily is the CEO and founder of EI & Company, where she and her team of home care experts provide Co-Leadership™ Services to home care owners. Their biggest success thus far has been helping a client improve operations and revenue by 650% in less than six months. EI & Company's goal is to always "teach a man to fish" and to ensure once they know how, EI & Company will get out of their way!

In addition to Co-Leadership services, Emily and her team of home care experts provide a variety of programs to franchisors. Their most successful being Powerhouse Peers™, a third-party-provided performance group program where franchisors utilize the expertise of EI & Company's years of home care success to build their franchisees businesses in a highly specialized performance group approach. Other programs offered include Profitable Performance™, an outsourced support team for coaching, consulting, and leadership development for franchisees, as well as a Revenue Reboot™ workshop for under-performing franchisees.

All of the services EI & Company provides allows franchisors to have peace of mind that they are not crossing the lines of joint employment and are mitigating risk with vicarious liability while also trusting their franchisees are receiving incredible advice on how to run their business well.

Emily can be reached at www.eiandcompany.com.